W9-CCY-041

DANGEROUS JOURNEY

DANGEROUS JOURNEY

ADVENTURES OF A YOUNG FAMILY
TRAVELING WEST IN 1799

C. B. MURRAY

authorHOUSE®

AuthorHouse™
1663 Liberty Drive
Bloomington, IN 47403
www.authorhouse.com
Phone: 1-800-839-8640

© 2012 by C. B. Murray. All rights reserved.

No part of this book may be reproduced, stored in a retrieval system, or transmitted by any means without the written permission of the author.

This is a work of fiction. All of the characters, names, incidents, organizations, and dialogue in this novel are either the products of the author's imagination or are used fictitiously.

Published by AuthorHouse   10/08/2012

ISBN: 978-1-4772-6928-2 (sc)
ISBN: 978-1-4772-6929-9 (hc)
ISBN: 978-1-4772-6930-5 (e)

Library of Congress Control Number: 2012917033

Any people depicted in stock imagery provided by Thinkstock are models, and such images are being used for illustrative purposes only.
Certain stock imagery © Thinkstock.

Because of the dynamic nature of the Internet, any web addresses or links contained in this book may have changed since publication and may no longer be valid. The views expressed in this work are solely those of the author and do not necessarily reflect the views of the publisher, and the publisher hereby disclaims any responsibility for them.

CONTENTS

DEDICATION

Richard, Ada and Annette

Acknowledgements

My especial gratitude goes to Richard Murray, as always my best friend and main support. Heartfelt thanks to Kate Ward, Ada Koch, and Annette Orella for reading the early manuscript, suggesting changes and corrections every step of the way and to internationally known artist, Ada Koch for the imaginative cover design and images that portray so faithfully the events and characters. Grateful acknowledgement is made to the team at Author House who prepared this book for publication.

CHAPTER ONE

A Fire in
the Schoolhouse

"**N**o, it's *my* turn! You promised! You had the sled yesterday. Today *I* get to go down Devil's Hill. Frank Littrell crowed I couldn't do it. He called me chicken! I just *have* to do it. I'm going to use the sled the whole recess after lunch."

"Why can't you do the easy hill, Lucy—and share?" Cyrus griped. "Why do you always want to do scary things? You're just like Pa! I heard him talking to Mr. Putnam and some of our other neighbors a few days ago. He wants us to move all the way out to Ohio. It isn't even a state, just a territory in the wilderness. People get killed going out there! We're safe and settled among folks right here in Vermont. Why can't he stay put? Why do you have to have the sled all the time!"

Our teacher, the Reverend Mr. Matthew Stacey, was looking at us as we walked into our one-room schoolhouse. My brother and I lowered our voices.

"Don't change the subject, Cyrus. And besides, I'm *eleven*! You're only ten," I hissed. "I'm stronger than you, and I'm going to take the sled! Anyway, you made a bargain. So there!" I stuck my tongue out.

"Wait and see! You'll be sorry!" Cyrus whispered.

"If I might have your attention!" Mr. Stacey struck his table smartly with a ruler and snapped in a no-nonsense voice, "Please hang up your coats and take your places."

All morning I looked up at the clock. The minute hand ticked slowly from one number to the next. What did Cyrus mean by "You'll be sorry?" I wondered. At lunchtime I gobbled my bread and meat and ran out the door. I didn't see Cyrus. Good, I thought, I won't have to fight him for the sled. I put on my woolen capote and mittens.

The sled was right where I had left it. That was odd. Cyrus hadn't even tried to hide it. Why? I grabbed the ropes and started dragging the heavy sled up Devil's Hill, the highest point near the school. The snow was deep in Poultney, Vermont, and it was hard pulling. When I finally reached the top, I looked down. It was a *long, long* way down. It's longer than I thought. I gulped and looked down again. No! I said I'd do it, and I will!

"Watch out! Here I come!" I yelled and threw myself on the hand sled Pa had made for us and headed pell-mell down Devil's Hill toward the schoolhouse. I felt the hard wooden slats against my ribs as I skidded over the crust of ice. Snowflakes pricked at my face like little pins and stung my nose and eyes. My fingers seemed frozen stiff. The wind whistled past me and made a whirring noise as I rocketed down and down. I loved that feeling! Whee! I was flying!

Suddenly, through the blur of snow and ice, I saw a huge boulder that looked like it was speeding toward me. I could see its ragged edges and gigantic hard sides. I screamed! The sled's guiding rod was frozen. Oh, no! I couldn't steer. Just as I was about to collide with that gleaming rock, I leaned to the right with all my might and held on tightly as the sled flipped up on one runner. In a panic, I tried to straighten the guide rod, and the sled ricocheted to the left. Where had that huge rock come from? It had never been there on the slope. My left foot grazed the stone's surface as I flew by. Whoosh! The sled veered off to the right, and I was headed toward some little children playing in the snow. "Move! Run! Get out of the way!" I screamed, "I can't stop the sled! Run! Run!. "I missed them by inches.

Momentum kept building. Faster. Faster. The sled was out of control and racing toward the schoolhouse. "Oh, no!" I wailed in terror. The building loomed higher and closer!

At that moment, Cyrus came around the side of the building. He grinned wickedly and flung the door open wide. Where had he come from? Why was he there? The sled bumped over the doorframe like it was on wheels, bounced on a loose floorboard. Splat! I fell off in a heap on the floor. Wham! The sled ran smack against the andirons in the fireplace. Logs jolted out of the pile, and hot embers scattered all over the floor. The school was on fire! A sour smell of wood smoke was all around me. Flames started licking up from the floor. Everyone began to scream and run away. Oh, no! What had I done?

"Fire! Fire!" Everyone screamed.

"Quick!" Mr. Stacey yelled. "Sweep the coals back into the fireplace! The school will burn down! Stamp on the embers!" The man madly dancing across the glowing coals in front of the fireplace looked more like one of our chickens lurching around the yard after Ma cut its head off than the calm Mr. Stacey we knew. All of my classmates looked scared, but they began jumping and running. They used jackets and brooms to swoosh the live coals and burning ash back into the grate. They tramped on sparks coming up from the dry wood. Dazed, I watched it all from a sprawl on the floor.

Finally, the last ember was squashed. Everyone was quiet, and they all were looking at me. I sat very still. "Miss Sophronia Howe!" Mr. Stacey wasn't using his fire and brimstone voice. His tone was softer than I had ever heard it . . . and much scarier. His forehead wrinkled, his eyebrows came together and soot flecked his cheeks. "Would you please explain yourself!

My limbs still splayed on the floor, I looked all the way up from his heavy boots, rough wool leggings and woolsey over-shirt to his scowling face with thin wisps of hair across his forehead. Already his bushy brows looked like storm clouds before the lightning, and his steely blue eyes looked down on me. Mr. Stacy was a busy farmer with little time for any kind of horseplay. He taught in our one-room school in the winter and gave hellfire sermons to the congregation at Hayden Chapel on the weekends. He had no time for cappers.

"I'm sorry, Mr. Stacey. When I steered around a boulder on the hill I could see I was heading right for some little kids and had to veer off toward the school to miss them. I didn't think about coming all the way in." I looked around and saw the smirk on Cyrus's face. I'd have bet anything right that minute that he'd got his friends and shoved that boulder in the way. That was just like him!

"Sorry won't do! You must start thinking before you act. Please take your place under the desk." I was stunned. I let my breath out slowly. I couldn't believe Mr. Stacey wasn't going to thrash me with the Old Persuader on the wall! Why wasn't he paddling me? Why did he let me off so easy?

As punishment, Mr. Stacey either thrashed with that paddle or made students sit under his desk. I had been under that table a good many times. I knew his shoes better than his face. There was a neat patch on the right boot toe. His left boot heel was worn at the outside. If I saw those boots walking down the street, I could call, "Hello, Mr. Stacey," without looking up to see a head.

As I crawled under the table, I tried to comfort myself. I thought sitting there was better than the hurt and shame of getting paddled before the class. I peeked out the side at Cyrus. I bet you did this! Wait until I get you on the way home, I thought. You'll be sorry! Cyrus smiled at me smugly.

While I sat cramped under the desk all afternoon, the younger students read at the front of the room. The older students did math on slates at their tables. I could hear their writing rocks scritching and scratching. Our family, like most of the others, couldn't afford chalk. The only two students in school who used it sat near me, and their chalk made loads of dust. I could taste it in my mouth. I smelled it in my nose. I sneezed.

When I peeked out, Cyrus had his tongue wedged between his teeth—a sign that he couldn't remember what he'd just wiped off his slate. He'd run his fingers through his hair so much it stood up like little spikes all over his head. Good, I thought, and felt better. Serves him right! I hope he gets called on next. I could memorize easily, and that thought helped me forget the crick in my neck.

Overhead, I heard Mr. Stacey sharpening quill pens with more than his usual vigor. He was mad, really mad!. The older students used quills to write essays. I smelled the ink of lampblack and oil. Some of the ink dripped through a crack in the desk and made a little pool at my feet. I tried to move quietly. I didn't want it to get on my skirt, and I didn't want to rile Mr. Stacey. I peeked around the legs of the table again. My older sister Sarah bit her lower lip, twisted a lock of corn-colored hair between her fingers and rocked back and forth on a three-legged stool while she copied a passage from the Bible. Our parents built all of the stools and tables, and, because there were nine children in our family, we handed down the stools Pa built.

I was stiff when school let out. It took me several minutes just to stand up straight. That gave Cyrus time to put on his blanket shirt and run half way up the hill toward home while I was still tying my capote and hood. He knew I was going to go after him before he got there. Neither Sarah nor my younger brother Thomas would tattle, but he'd blab to Ma. Of all my eight brothers and sisters, Cyrus was the worst!

Light was fading fast, and I barely could pick out Cyrus's shadow against the top of the snow-covered hill. Sarah and Thomas were trailing behind him. Big white flakes began drifting from the sky, so I didn't stop to listen to the scary silence that always came with a new snowfall. I was going at a fast trot and was ready to catch that traitor by the scuff of his neck when Cyrus yelled, "Stop! What's *this*?" We all gathered 'round to see what he was pointing to in the snow. Outlined in the powdery whiteness was a huge set of tracks. They marched down the hill and crossed the road, and wandered off across the meadow.

"What makes that kind of a footprint?" Sarah asked. "There's just one set of tracks. Do you suppose another animal is coming along?" Sarah took Thomas's hand. She was thirteen years old and always knew what to do. "I think we'd better hurry and all stay together!"

I tried to decide. I wanted to beat up Cyrus there in the snow, but what if some huge bear or gigantic wolf came after us? What if it saw Cyrus getting a thrashing and tried to help him? The bear might not understand that my little toad of a brother had it coming. He might take Cyrus's part. So I decided to be a good heart. I'd get closer to home, then I'd do him in. But he got home before I could catch him.

"Ma! Pa!" we shouted, each of us pushing and shoving, trying to be first to get in the house. "Guess what we saw?"

Pa sat at the table. He had finished the milking early. He pulled closer to the fire to see the print on the newspaper he held, his gray hair fell down over his forehead. Ma stirred soup in an iron kettle hanging from a crane in the fireplace. She reached up to tuck a lock of hair back into the bun at the nape of her neck.

Cyrus crowed with self-importance, "I found it first. It was a huge paw print!"

Pa was a hunter. He put down the paper right away and asked, "What did the track look like?"

"Well!" Cyrus puffed out his chest and all but swaggered. "It was twenty or twenty-five inches long! It wasn't as wide as it was long. It ran out to a point at the heel. Oh, and it was checks-like all over," he finished, nearly out of breath with excitement.

Ma looked at Pa her brown eyes bright and tried not to smile. Pa let out a huge guffaw! "Law, boy, somebody's been along there with snowshoes!"

Well! I can tell you that made me feel good. My, but I did enjoy his sheepish look. As we hung our coats on the hooks by the door, I whispered to Cyrus, "I knew that all along. You were so mean and guilty and running off. Otherwise, I would have told you and you wouldn't have made a jackass of yourself!" Of course, I didn't really know about snowshoes, but I'd never tell Cyrus that! He pulled my pigtails, and ran away, red-faced.

"Please do your chores before supper." Ma's voice sounded tired, and I remembered that she'd had a hard time eating lately. She upchucked most of her food every morning. Pa looked thoughtful, reached over and patted her hand. He stood to put more wood on the fire.

My older sisters Abby, the organizer, Becky, the flirt, and Minerva, the smart one, had been weaving cloth all day. They jumped up from the looms and the spinning wheel and started setting out supper.

"You young 'uns refill the porch woodpile," Abby called to the rest of us.

While Cyrus and Pa split logs, Thomas helped Sarah and me pile heaps of split wood by the porch door. When Pa and the boys went to wash up, Sarah and I carried a bundle of sticks and a few of the logs inside to stack by the fireplace.

The fireside was the center of our gathering room. Pa had made a large hearth of the smoothest, most regular stones we could find. They had been laid several feet into the room. A brick flue led up the chimney to the sky. As I placed the fresh-cut wood by the hearth, I was entranced for a moment by the roaring blaze in the huge fireplace. The light from this fire lit and heated the whole room so we didn't need candles.

The backlog that anchored the black andirons was about four feet long and two feet wide and seemed to birth the blood-orange flames that curled up and over another log about two-thirds its size. The fore-stick, about a foot in diameter, suddenly shifted on its perch at the front of the andirons, and a few sparks popped out onto the hearth, reminding me of the near disaster at school that day. I quickly dropped a smaller log between the fore and back logs—where we piled kindling each morning to arouse the banked fire—opened the iron door of the small baking oven at the side of the fireplace and removed the cornbread.

Abby and Becky placed two-quart pewter basins filled with bean soup, pewter platters laden with cracklin' cornbread and tankards of fresh milk on several stools and set beer on the table for Pa. We children knelt around the stools with our spoons and ate soup from the same basin. We shared bread from the platters and drank the warm milk.

Abby fed two-year-old Eva and patted Eva's brown ringlets between bites. She, Becky and Minerva sat around one stool. "I spun the most today," Becky boasted. "*And* I wove a whole yard of cloth." Her yellow curls bobbed saucily.

With a scornful little smile, Minerva broke off some cornbread and boasted, "True, but I wove most yesterday. You've never caught up with my two-and-a-half yards."

Sarah, with a fine line of milk above her cupid's-bow lips, whispered, "Mr. Stacey asked how you were, Abby. I think he likes you."

"Ha, ha. Abby has a sweetheart! Abby has a sweetheart!" Cyrus sang and choked on his cornbread!

Abby tossed her head and sniffed.

Becky joined in. "If I couldn't do better than that old woman in knickers, I'd be happy to stay an old maid."

Minerva's brown eyes danced, "Maybe that's why you don't have a sweetheart, Becky, you can't do better."

"Enough!" Pa didn't like family squabbling. "At eighteen, Abby is in no danger of spinsterhood. Stacey is a good man, hard working and sober. Becky, you would be better off putting your mind to weaving. Ma told me you girls turned out nearly eighty yards of linen and wool last year, thank the good Lord. We'll get income by selling what we don't use. Now, tell me what you learned in school today."

I held my breath and thought, here it comes. Sure to Betsy it did! Smirking, Cyrus began: "Well, we did have some excitement. Sophronia took that sled you made us down Devil's Hill. She shot right into the schoolhouse, and when the sled banged into the fireplace, sparks went all over the floor. She set the schoolhouse on fire! We all had to stomp out the fire, but we did it! Boy, was Mr.

Stacey ever mad. Serves her right! She wouldn't share the sled! I wish she'd banged into that rock!"

Ma put her hand over her heart as she caught her breath. "Land o'Goshen! You did what!? Lordy, you could have burned down the school!"

Pa just threw back his head. He laughed so hard his eyes watered. "Did I ever tell you about taking my Pa's horse? I spurred it so hard it bolted. That old nag was tied to a fence, and when we took off, most of that fence did too. What a paddlin' I got. I tell you, I couldn't sit down for a week." He wiped his eyes with the back of his hand.

"Are you going to paddle Sophronia? Are you Pa?" Cyrus clapped his hands.

Pa looked at me for a long minute. I felt my face burning. "Well now, Lucy," he whispered softly, using his pet name for me, "how did that come about?"

I stuttered, "You see, um, well . . . I started down the hill. Right in the way, half way down, I saw this huge boulder. I'd never seen it before. I had to pull off hard to miss it. When I steered back in the other direction so I wouldn't run into some little children, I was going so fast I lost control. I was headed right for the schoolhouse door. Cyrus was standing there. He opened the door, and I went right on in. But they got the fire out. Mr. Stacey sat me under the desk as punishment." I hung my head.

Pa rubbed his chin and just thought for a long minute. "I don't remember any boulders on that hill. I walked over there just last week when I went to the school board meeting. I thought what a good sledding hill it was. Come to think of it, I saw some pretty big boulders up on the bluff at Perry Heights. I reckon a bunch of boys with a tree limb as a lever could've pried one loose, and it would have dropped right down on the narrow part of Devil's Hill." He looked at Cyrus for another long minute. "And you were watching for her, you knew about the boulder and you opened the door?"

"Well, Pa, I saw her coming. I was afraid she'd bang into the door!" It wasn't just me who thought his explanation was rather lame. Everyone was silent looking at Cyrus. It was Cyrus's turn to redden as he realized he'd been caught out.

Ma stood up but sat back down again hard. Pa gave her a worried glance. Still seated, she spoke quietly, "You children don't realize how serious this is. If that school house had of caught fire, some children could have died. Mr. Stacey thought fast and saved you all. Lucy, it looks like however it happened you were punished. We'll speak of it no more." Her eyes narrowed and she began nodding her head slowly as she looked at Cyrus. "Young man, you were conveniently there to open the door. You and I will talk about this later." Cyrus squirmed. We all were quiet, we would rather have a thrashing than one of Ma's "talks." "I wish Mr. Stacey would use the paddle," she remarked. "That under-the-desk treatment could harm a child's spine!"

Abby quietly spoke up. "And using the Old Persuader wouldn't?"

Ma ignored the question. "Abby, please get Eva ready for bed. Eliza and Squire Prouty are coming over this evening. We'll have some cider and apple dumplings. Children, get cleaned up. Wait to put on your nightclothes until after they leave. Becky and Minerva, please help me with the dishes." She rose, and I breathed a sigh of relief.

I felt glad that Cyrus had his comeuppance, and I couldn't wait to see Eliza. At twenty, she was my oldest sister and had been married to Squire Ezra Prouty for two years. Short, with blue eyes, black curls and a happy disposition, she would liven up everybody,

We scrambled up the ladder to our sleeping quarters in the loft. That's where we stored our shoes and our few belongings. I was behind Cyrus and pinched him. I ran into the girls' section of the loft. He couldn't get me there! I stayed in the loft.

Soon I heard Eliza laughing. I waited to be sure Cyrus was down the ladder, and I dashed down and waited in line to kiss her.

"It's a beautiful night with a full moon. We just walked, it's not that far and we didn't need our lantern," Eliza sighed as she set it by the door. "The moon lit the way."

Squire Prouty shook hands all around and settled in by the fire next to Pa folding his hands over his pop belly. We children sat on the floor by the hearth and waited. Holding little Eva in her lap, Ma sat in the rocking chair Pa had built for her. Pa and the Squire shared a tankard of home-brewed beer while we children sipped cider pressed from apples we'd picked from the gnarly trees in our side yard.

"I got a letter from Josiah Hale today," Squire mumbled, he reached over and took a long drink before passing the tankard back to Pa. "They seem quite happy in the far west of Ohio. Seems to be good land, and the settlers are homesteading some large tracts. They had no trouble with the Indians."

Ma's eyes widened, and she grew very still. The Hales had spent four months on the trail to Ohio. Other settlers had told us tales of Indian attacks.

Pa wasn't scared of the Indians. He often talked to those who came around. "My great-great-grandpa, John Howe, was the first white settler in Marlborough, Massachusetts," Pa recounted. "He took the freeman's oath in 1640 and was surnamed The Just by the Indians. Once, two Indians were fightin' over a squash. The vine was in one's yard. The squash was on the other's land. When they sought out Grandpa Howe, who lived among them at that time, he called for a knife. He split that squash right down the middle and gave each Indian half a squash. From then on, they chose John the Just to sort out all their quarrels. No, I have no fear of the red man. After all," Pa paused as he stroked his chin, "they were here first."

Abby, had heard the story many times. She spoke quietly from her seat by the door. "But, Pa, you told us one of John Howe's twelve children, your great-grandpa John, was killed by the Indians in 1675. His little son Peter, your grandfather, was only four years old at the time! Lots of folk fear the Indians . . . for good reason."

Pa shook his head. "Every group has some bad 'uns."

Silence blanketed the room. Squire Prouty soon picked up the conversation though. Once he started to worry a subject, he couldn't be stopped. "Well, I was thinking and talking to Eliza. Wouldn't it be advantageous to try our luck? Maybe we could go out to Ohio. We could sign up for some of that cheap land. It won't last for ever."

So that was why they had come! The Squire, who owned a farm and had a blacksmith's shed, always had an eye out for a good buy. Something upset me about the look Ma and Pa had exchanged. I could tell Pa was getting excited. But Ma had pressed her lips into a straight line. She did that when she was holding her temper. I don't think she liked the idea.

"Well," the Squire continued, "it was just a thought. Something we can cogitate over this spring. Don't have to decide right away. If we wait too long, though, all the good land's gone." He took another draft from the tankard. I liked the words "advantageous" and "cogitate." I wondered what they meant. I'd ask Minerva.

In her lovely, soft voice, Eliza cut in, for she had seen the look between Ma and Pa that the Squire had missed. "Pa, I think Prouty would like to hear a story. The one about the Hessian soldier after the Battle of Bennington."

Immediately we all yelled, "Oh, Yes! Do tell!" That was the best one of all. The Squire had heard the story many times too, but he was not totally dense. He understood all talk of Ohio was to be put on hold.

"Wait!" I begged. "I want to hear about the Battle of Breed's Hill. You were there, Pa. Tell us, please!"

"Well, if you're sure you want to hear it . . ." Pa leaned down and patted me on the head as he settled back.

"Were those battles as dangerous as going out to Ohio with all the Indians and wild animals will be, Pa? Lots of people have died from Indian raids and wolves attacking at night. And the bears are huge and snakes are all around the swamps and rivers. Some people have drowned trying to forge the rivers or their canoes have turned over. Could we die if we go to Ohio?" Cyrus asked all excited, his face red from the fire. Pa shot a look at Ma who had uttered a little cry.

Eliza had heard Ma's little gasp and she spoke in a voice unusually sharp, "Cyrus, do you want to hear the war stories and have some goodies or do you want to go up to bed?" Eliza always knew how to shut Cyrus up.

We all chanted "Story, story!' We hugged our knees and waited.

CHAPTER TWO

AN ENEMY
HESSIAN SOLDIER

The good smell of soup was still in the air, and I sniffed the promise of fresh apple pudding. We put off the fear of an Ohio trip. Everything was right and safe, and we were eager to hear of Pa's adventure. Whenever he told us stories, we felt we were traveling to another place. He had been there. He had faced the Brits and their guns. At first his words came slowly, as though he'd pulled them up from a long-forgotten well, and they bubbled to the top and burst into the daylight.

Firelight shown on our faces as Pa began the story in a low voice: "I'll never forget the day I signed up with Captain Cyprian Howe's company in the Marlborough Regiment. It was April 19, 1775, and most of us farmers had been out getting the fields ready for planting when we heard the British were marching on Concord. I think we were all a little unnerved by the news, as we had arms stored there. Gen. Thomas Gage thought his march was a secret. What a laugh." Pa's eyes twinkled, and he grinned. "Boston was like an open book. Everybody knew what everyone else was having for supper. General

Gage put British soldiers in boats to cross the Charles River, march fifteen miles to Concord. We didn't need Paul Revere to shout out the news. Church bells were ringing all along the way to warn us the Brits were coming. We all grabbed our guns and took off from our fields and homes.

"Now some things I won't support. I've never had much sympathy for Boston hotheads. I think they started the Boston Massacre. We didn't have any local policemen or sheriffs in Massachusetts, so we relied on English soldiers to keep the peace. One day some drunken roustabouts came straight out of a tavern and began throwing stones and bricks. Shots were fired. Boston accused the Brits of unlawful shooting, but the soldiers were only defending themselves from a mob! My hat's off to John Adams for having the courage to state that the British soldiers were just doing their duty.

"But that Concord business was different. Things weren't settled like they are now, and the British planned to take our rifles and gunpowder. As Abby just reminded us, some bad Indians killed my great granddaddy. They also killed one of my aunts and kidnapped another. We needed those guns for hunting food and for our protection, and we wanted to keep what was ours. So, at nineteen, about the same age as you, Abby, and full of bravado, I set off for Concord with my Pa and some relatives.

"The other farmers who joined us to face down the Brits couldn't resist ribbing the men in our family. Our name was Howe, and an English general had the same name. But there were sixteen of us Howes, and we were hefty men. No one had the nerve to do more than laugh. They teased a little, but we took it kindly.

"All of the snow had melted from the little stream at Concord's North Bridge, where I took my stand. It was a lovely spring morning. The flowers were just beginning to bloom, and I could smell the wet earth.

"Maj. John Pitcairn and Col. Francis Smith, who led the Brits, met the American militia at Lexington, just a few miles up the road from Concord. Major Pitcairn ordered his men to surround and disarm the militia. Capt. John Parker, leading the America militia, no sooner gave an order to disperse than some stupid, trigger-happy idiot fired that first shot. The Brits fired, killing eight Colonials and wounding ten. Our militia, already prepared to disperse, ran for cover in the woods. How would you have felt looking down a musket barrel, knowing it had already killed the man next to you?"

Pa's voice held a sharper edge as he continued. The firelight played over his forehead and cheeks and showed an angry man. "We were stunned! We were just defending our property and didn't really think the British would fire on their own countrymen. Yes, children, we were all still subjects of the King of England. That shooting, though, stiffened a lot of spines

"Seven hundred Brits, with muskets, bayonets and light guns, moved on to Concord. We had muskets and blunderbusses. Some just had any weapon they could lay hands on—clubs, pitchforks and the like. Warned that the Redcoats were on their way, the citizens of Concord carried off most of the stores before Colonel Smith got there. The Brits found and took gun carriages, entrenching tools, flour and a liberty pole. They destroyed what was left and spread out to find cannons. They'd heard some were secreted at Barrett's farm. Well, we were ready for them. We met them at North Bridge. They fired shots. We returned fire and drove them back. We shot fourteen Brits. They left that bridge fast enough and started back to Boston. They burned and looted Colonials' homes along the way. I heard they caught and executed several colonial militia good men and true, poor devils.

"So the English started back to Boston. Up to that time, no British soldiers had been killed. We took places along the way. A militiaman stood behind every tree and rock. We fought Indian style. Lots more recruits were joining us. Shooting Redcoats was like picking off birds at a turkey shoot. Took 'em all by surprise. They were used to lining up and marching right up to the enemy. They'd start shooting face-to-face. Of all the damn ways . . . oh sorry, Orinda," he darted a look at Ma. "I mean stupid ways to fight! "We squirmed in our seats.

"Those Englishmen were out-numbered and scared silly. The only thing that saved their skins was that Brig. Gen. Hugh Percy, with 600 men under his command, set out from Boston six hours after Colonel Smith and was waiting at Lexington with two cannons that he fired straightaway at the Colonials. By gum, you don't argue with a cannon. Percy reorganized the British troops and started back to Boston. They took heavy fire from us all along the way. We didn't lose over 90 men, but I heard 19 officers and 250 Brits were killed or wounded. That, of course, led to the colonist's Siege of Boston and the beginning of the American Revolutionary War."

"Good show, Pa." Cyrus waved his hands in the air and shouted. Our faces were red from excitement, and even Squire Prouty seemed fascinated.

Ma spoke up, "I think that's enough war for one night. All this talk of killing! The children will never be able to sleep."

"Oh, no, Ma! Just one more story! It's still early." We all pleaded.

Eliza smiled. She loved Pa's war stories. "Maybe we could have a break," she suggested. "I'd like to sample your apple tart, Ma,"

Ma was proud of her cooking for good reason. She'd spent a goodly time making the tart, and we hadn't had a chance to taste it.

"Well, just one more story after dessert." I noticed Ma rose with some difficulty. Eliza noticed too, and she jumped up to help Ma cut the tart. They put a small piece in each of our hands.

"You've outdone yourself, Ma. This is just delicious," Eliza praised with a worried look toward Ma.

Ma smiled, well pleased, and sank into her rocker.

"Go on, Pa. Tell us about Bunker Hill and Bennington!"

"After Concord most of us went home to put in crops. But, Boston was under siege, so, in June of '75, we went back to fight in the Battle of Bunker Hill, although the battle actually took place on Breed's Hill. I'm one of the lucky ones who lived to tell about it. I was just nineteen, as I said, but we were all inexperienced. Only this time I'd seen men killed at Concord. My bravado was gone, and I was half-scared to death.

"The Committee of Safety wanted to encircle the British in Boston. To do that we'd have to control Breed's *and* Bunker hills. On the sixteenth of June, Maj. Israel Putnam and Col. William Prescott led men with only one day's provisions and blankets up Breed's Hill under cover of dark. Silently we started to put up fortifications. We dug trenches and put up bales of cotton and hay on Breeds hill. The breastworks were ten rods long and eight wide. Putnam took some men and started fortifying Bunker Hill. Good thing he did.

"Imagine General Gage's surprise when he looked up early in the morning to see that the Americans had fortified the hills! Gage sent out orders. 'Ships in the harbor! Ships in the ferry way and in the river! Bomb the hills!' Their shelling covered British soldiers moving up the hill and kept us from getting reinforcements.

"About three in the afternoon, a sentinel called out. 'Forty barges and boats coming loaded with 3,000 British soldiers!' We numbered but 700 with 500 reinforcements. We were terrified! Some of the younger recruits turned tail and ran. Can't say I blamed 'em. From our lookout we could see it all. British Regulars marched from Boston to Charleston, plundering and burning.

"Gage ordered ship's cannons to fire incendiary shells to Charlestown. I tell you," Pa whispered, his eyes all hollow as though seeing it unfold all over again, "Charlestown went up in flames. The wooden church steeples were huge pillars of fire. You could hear the roar of cannons and mortars. Whole streets full of buildings fell, smoldering and flaring, and large clouds of black smoke choked us. That was the most hellish of all the battles I've seen.

"Through the smoke we could see Boston. Thousands of spectators crowded churches, housetops and shore batteries watching the encounter. To them, it was a clear summer day. They could see perfectly.

"General Howe was late sending in his men, so our militia had time to put up a barrier of post-and-rail fences. A company of New Hampshire riflemen who could hit a halfpenny at fifty yards stood by the breastworks.

"The first charge was split. Some British troops pushed to the east of Breed's Hill. A second group came charging straight up. Well, tired as we were, our boys fought. We just mowed 'em down. As we were low on ammunition, the order rang out: 'Don't fire 'til you see the whites of their eyes.' When they were but fifty yards from the barricade, we let go a volley. The Redcoats collapsed and lay in heaps, wounded and dead. I'll be darned; they retreated. That really cheered us up.

"But the British soldiers were experienced and professional, and their officers were ambitious. So the second attack came. Like the first, that one failed also. General Howe was steaming and ordered a third attack. His men tossed their heavy packs and used their bayonets! Our ammunition was low. My muscles ached; the sweat was pouring down my face getting in my eyes so I had to keep swiping to see where to shoot. I was afraid I'd drop my gun 'cause my hands were so wet from sweat. We had only the arms we'd carried up with us, so we had to withdraw. The reserves were to go forward and replace the front line, but some soldiers confused 'fall back' with 'retreat'. Things got muddled. Remember, though, that General Putnam put up some fortifications on Bunker Hill. He covered our retreat brilliantly."

Disappointed, Cyrus asked, "But, does that mean the British won?"

Pa leaned forward in his chair. "Well, son, I guess by the rules of war they won. For the time being, they'd gained control of the heights over Boston. But look at it this way. They lost forty percent of their men. That's over a thousand! We lost about 450 with 30 captured. The main thing is that the British army—the greatest in the world—was vulnerable. They retreated twice before a small, inexperienced corps of lightly-armed militiamen. I'd call that a moral victory! Now you take Bennington. That was a just-plain-no-questions-asked victory!"

"Would anyone like more dessert?" Ma interrupted. "I'm going to put Eva down. It's late for a two-year-old." Ma had given up trying to derail Pa's recounting. She knew when family opinion was too strong to fight. She picked her battles.

"Let me, Ma." Eliza jumped to her feet, giving Abby and Becky a steely stare. "You've done enough for today, let *us* help you." Gently picking up Eva, already half-asleep, Eliza carried her to our parents' room. As we watched through the open door, she removed Eva's bodice and cap, and the little girl curled up in the wooden cradle at foot of Ma's bed.

Abby gave Becky a nudge. "I'd like some more dessert. Pa's stories always make me hungry."

As Becky rose, she snapped, "Everything makes you hungry, Abby. If you're not careful, you'll be as fat as . . ."

"Girls!" Pa scolded sternly. He hated family fighting, which always struck me strange, because he seemed to relish retelling his war stories. But something else was happening. Looks were exchanged among Eliza, Abby and Becky. They had some secret. I vowed to ask Sarah or Minerva later. Maybe they knew what was going on.

With Eva tucked in, Eliza returned to the hearth. Abby had served everyone and sat down. I found it hard to think of war as I sat by the warm fire with family all around, but Pa's voice guided me back to the battlefield

"In the spring of 1777, nearly a year after the Declaration of Independence had been signed, the British had a plan to separate New England from the southern and central colonies. Maj. Gen. John Burgoyne, known as 'Gentleman Johnny,' was to move south from Ticonderoga, New York. He'd go from Lake Champlain overland to the Hudson and meet up with Howe marching northward from New York City. Together they'd capture Albany. Had the plan worked, I'd have been hung and long dead, and you'd be subjects of the British Crown." No one dared point out that if he had died, we wouldn't be here at all!

"General Burgoyne captured Fort Ticonderoga, near the south end of Lake Champlain, and felt very proud of himself. He offered pardon to everyone who would join him. Some did. But he made two mistakes. First he'd set Iroquois on those not joining him. Second, he used Hessian troops in his army, and that turned public opinion against him. I can understand why the Indians might attack colonists at the urging of the British. Americans were taking their land without a treaty. That's always bothered me. But to hire foreign troops to fight us! Because they still maintained we were English, that just didn't sit right with me or other folks. As so many of the troops forced into military service and hired out to the British for low pay came from the state of Hesse in Germany, we called all conscripted soldiers fighting against us 'Hessians.'

'Things began to look bad for us. We hadn't won any decisive battles, and not France nor Spain would help us. But things didn't look so great for Gentleman Johnny either. Burgoyne was low on supplies, and he had a hard time moving his troops. The 10,000 soldiers, 3,000 Canadian loyalists and 400 Indian scouts as well as 2,000 women and children stretched out in a line well over a mile long. Does it surprise you that families often traveled with their men during wartime?" Pa asked. "The women provided a lot of useful services. They mended, cooked, took care of the sick and did laundry."

"Just like at home!" Minerva commented. Everyone laughed.

"I almost felt sorry for Burgoyne," Pa continued. "He had to feed and take care of that whole menagerie as they traveled through more than twenty miles of heavy undergrowth and swamp. All the while, the Americans tormented his troops, sniping at them and burning bridges. I think the Brits were surprised that so many locals were armed. You see, English farmers aren't allowed to carry muskets.

"At first the Brits moved one mile a day, but as the trip progressed, they made one mile a week. Also, it was brutally hot that July. Those men wore heavy wool uniforms, and the flies and mosquitoes were ravenous near those swamps. Yes, siree, they were not happy." He laughed. "Speaking of hot, Cyrus and Thomas, please add logs to the fire?" They both jumped up and got some wood. Cyrus sneaked another apple tart before they sat down again.

Pa continued. "All our men were joining up to fight. When news came back here to Poultney that the British had taken Hubbardton, only twelve miles and a day's march away, the women folk and children were in church. Without the protection of husbands, fathers and brothers, who were off skirmishing, some of them just picked up and left without going back home. The only lady with a horse was Mrs. Marshall, who had nine youngsters. She rode while her children walked along with the others. That day the women walked fifteen miles south to Pawlet. Willard's Tavern turned them away, so over the next days they walked another forty miles to Bennington, where their men folk returning from fighting found their families worn out and hungry.

"Burgoyne heard rumors of large herds of horses at Bennington. Thinking the town was poorly guarded, he sent Lt. Col. Friedrich Baum with German soldiers there for horses. The men of Poultney, still in Bennington with their families, got word Hessians were coming. Thirteen women with their children set off for Pownal, ten miles further down the road. My Ma and aunt were among them. They finally made it to safety in Massachusetts and Connecticut. Those brave women came back the next fall with their children to face again possible fighting and dying. They are true heroines. We'll always remember them.

"Although hot as blazes that August day in '77, we Vermont soldiers were ready to fight! We'd had a stomach full of the English and their hired guns! The number of militia at Bennington really surprised Colonel Baum, begorra! Our men succeeded in breaking the corps! Baum was wounded and left on the field, and we had the Hessians running into the woods. Would you believe that when we followed them into the trees, we ran into five hundred grenadiers and light infantry! Lt. Col. Heinrich von Breyman had come to assist Baum.

"I can tell you we were winded and tired, but just then our prayers were answered! Col. Seth Warner and his veteran Green Mountain Boys turned up right at that moment, loaded with guns they'd found! Seems Col. Enoch Hale's New Hampshire militiamen had stacked arms near Hubbardton's woods. We let out a war whoop that'd scare an Indian. We took off chasing every Redcoat we could see. That battle lasted until sunset. The Brits lost four cannons and 1,000 muskets. Worse for them, they had 200 dead and 750 wounded. Our toll was 30 killed, 40 wounded."

Pa sat silently and stared at the fire. We waited. We knew the best part was coming. When he continued, his voice had lost its vigor and enthusiasm. He wiped his forehead several times with his hand. "The sun was setting, and we couldn't see well," he continued at last. "We had to give up chasing the enemy. Although we were ready to collapse, we had to meet up with the other soldiers. As we picked our way past the dead, the fellows up front saw a wounded enemy soldier. The Hessian had raised his head up against a tree. He was motioning to his water canteen, speaking German. A man in the front line stopped and bellowed, 'I can't speak German! We don't want you here!' You won't believe this, but that bully shot the Hessian again. He shot a wounded man sitting on the ground! The German fell over. When we got to him, he was still breathing, so I tried to give him water from my canteen. It ran down his face, but he got a little. I gave my gun to my Pa. Several men picked up that wounded soldier and draped him over my shoulders. He was a right hefty load, and I was dead tired. Just the same, we made it back to camp. We could hear the wolves, and the coyotes howling. They were calling to their pack: 'Come feast on the dead and wounded.' A real eerie sound, I can hear it still!

"We didn't have a stockade for prisoners, so we took the Hessian to a double-log house of a farmer who brought nurses and Dr. Jacob Roebeck, a surgeon, to tend to the Hessian. When we went for a drink at the barracks, the bully who had shot the Hessian simply for spite was boasting, 'Well, I put one damned Hessian out of his misery.' Imagine bragging about shooting a defenseless, wounded man!" Pa paused, his eyes narrow and angry. "Later, I shared my rations with that Hessian, and we moved off." Pa shook his head, sat and stared at his hands. He forgot all of us waiting for the ending. Ma coughed and Pa looked up at our faces. "Well, the Indians and

Canadians eventually deserted Burgoyne. That fall the American forces under Gates and Benedict Arnold soundly whomped him at Saratoga. General Arnold was the real hero of the day, and, in mid-October, Gentleman Johnny surrendered his whole blasted army. Nearly 5,000 men!

Ma got to her feet. "I think we really have to stop now. Eliza has a far piece to walk back home." Everyone stood up and began their goodnights and good-byes. I went over to Pa.

Looking at Cyrus, I spit out angrily, "Some people deserve to be shot!"

Pa looked up. "Cyrus won't hound you if you don't pinch him going up the ladder."

I hung my head. Pa never missed a thing. I waited a moment so as to at least appear guilty and sorry even if I wasn't! I asked, "So, why did you save that Hessian? Maybe an Englishman I could understand. But that German was a foreign enemy. I don't understand!"

Pa took my hand. "Honey, I'm sorry to hear you say that. He was a wounded human being in a strange place. He didn't even speak our language! Maybe, I can justify killing someone who's going to kill me. Just maybe. But human dignity demands you don't hurt a wounded somebody in such a dire state."

I wondered, as I climbed the ladder, if I would have helped him. I wasn't sure.

CHAPTER THREE

A PECULIAR
PUNISHMENT

"For heaven's sake, wake up!" Minerva was shaking me. We had gone to bed late with the story telling. I didn't want to leave the warm bed. I was all snuggled up under the comforter. "It's Saturday, so no school. We're going to bake and brew today. Cyrus and Thomas have built a fire. The oven by the fireplace is heated. We've all eaten breakfast. So, your highness, please come down. We could use your help."

Minerva was not usually mean. I guessed she had been wakened before me. She probably had done the milking already and was angry to see me lying there. It was cold, so my stockings were on in a minute. And as we all slept in our chemises, I quickly put my gown and bodice over it, tied my apron and followed her down the ladder.

The grown-ups had eaten long since. Some meat was left on a plate for me. A mug of thyme tea sat cooling by the plate. "Sleepy head. Eating with the babies!" jeered Cyrus as I scorched a crust of bread. "We'll call you Miss Lazy Bones. I've built a fire in the oven, so there. It's hot enough for Abby to put in the bread!" Cyrus face, red from the fire, showed up the freckles from his forehead to his chin.

Our oven was in the chimney by the fireplace. The fire had heated the oven's brick lining. Cyrus propped open the oven door. With a short shovel, he removed the ashes. I could feel the oven's heat on my face all the way over at the table.

Abby must have been up before dawn. The heat from the fire was intense, and she was standing right by it. Her auburn hair hung in damp curls around her face. She didn't take my part as she sometimes did. I guessed she, too, was miffed that I'd overslept.

Our bread was made of corn and rye meal. Abby already had mixed the dough and let it rise. After she kneaded it down, she formed six loaves with her hands. With a wooden paddle, she shoved each loaf into the oven until all six were in. Her temper flared as she slammed the door shut.

"Cyrus, Pa wants you to help him with the brewing. Lucy, when you finish eating, feed the chickens. Next you can spool and quill the yarn."

I waited until Cyrus had left. "Where is Ma?"

"She's lying down. Not feeling too well this morning." Abby started to mix up another batch of bread.

"Abby, could I ask you a question? I've noticed that Ma hasn't been feeling well. She's all weak and upchucking. I saw you and Eliza exchange funny looks last night. Is Ma sick? Is she going to die?" The question had been in my mind all night. Speaking out loud brought the fears out in the open. I held back tears.

Abby turned to stare at me. She wiped her hands on her apron, came over and sat down by me. She stroked my hair. "Little Lucy, is that what's been bothering you? No, Honey, Ma's not going to die. She's going to have a baby. When a woman's in the family way, she can't keep food down. She'll be all right real soon. I think the baby is due around August."

For some reason, I started to cry. I don't know why. That Ma had given birth to Cyrus, Thomas and Eva I didn't mind. This time, though, I began to understand that only girls had babies. This time seemed more personal. Plus I felt stupid. I knew rams and bulls never had babies. Why hadn't I made the connection to humans?

Cyrus came in and stared at me. As we never cried, it may be that he was embarrassed by my tears and didn't know what to do. So he chanted, "What's the matter, cry baby? Didn't you get enough sleep?"

Gentle Abby turned on him with a fury. We'd never seen her that mad before. Both of us stared at her dumbfounded. She grabbed him by the ear. "Cyrus, I told you to go help with the brewing. If I catch you eavesdropping again, I'll thrash you good! Now, git!"

She handed me a tin basin. "You go get this filled with corn and feed the chickens. You'll feel better if you get some fresh air."

I put on my capote and went to the barn. Corn for chickens was stored there in large barrels. I filled the basin, went out and started calling, "Heeere, chick. Here, chick, chick, chick." As some of the hens had wandered over toward the woods, I followed them, leaving a trail of corn. I heard a strange bawling from the trees that sounded like a sheep in distress. I guess Cyrus heard it too. He came running as I started for the woods. "Wait for me, Lucy! It could be a wolf got a sheep!"

Together we tiptoed into the trees, going deeper and deeper into the forest. Trees were dripping icicles. The ground was still covered in snow. We didn't see any wolf tracks, but up ahead we spotted an ewe lying on the ground. She was bleating and heaving. We crept over beside her and hunched down. With three more pitiful cries, she had a spasm. We saw she was birthing. A little lamb no bigger than a kitten came squirming out. It was all covered with a film. I had seen birthing before, but this was different. For some reason I started to cry again. Cyrus looked awkwardly over at me. "It's all right, Lucy. She's going to be just fine."

"How do you know?" I shouted. "I bet it hurts her a lot. Else she wouldn't be wailing." I felt bad when I saw his hurt look. I reached over and patted his arm. "I'm sorry. You were trying to make me feel better. I don't know what's wrong with me. I guess I'm just feeling crotchety today."

Pa and Becky came up behind us. They must have heard the racket. "My, oh, my. The birthing is starting early this year," Pa lamented. "We're going to have to get them into the barn. We'll need to keep this mama warm. She can nurse the young one. Cyrus, you and Lucy help Becky. Go out and round up those other ewes. Try to get them to the barn, and I'll take care of this 'un." Our sheep were the size of dogs. They ran wild in the woods, only coming to the barnyard for salt. I could see we would spend a good many hours out rounding them all up; but if we didn't, they would freeze and the lambs would die out in the forest.

Every farmer put his own brand on the ears of his sheep. We could tell our sheep by the one overbite notch on the left ear. Pa usually kept one ram and twenty ewes. He swapped the rams with neighbors for breeding. Some of the wethers were slaughtered for mutton when they got to the right size—about thirty-to-forty pounds. It generally took two years to get full grown. There was no way to preserve lamb meat like there is for pork or beef, so as a rule we killed sheep and ate mutton in the spring.

We always had our big meal in the middle of the day. When we came in for dinner just after the noon hour, the aroma was pure heaven. A large piece of pork had cooked in the kettle on the crane over the fire all morning. Ma had put a corn pudding in a sack in the pot. She'd added potatoes, cabbage and carrots in the last few hours. When all was done, she dished the pudding out on a large pewter platter and the rest of the victuals on another platter. We set the table with pewter plates and wooden trenchers, and Ma put a quart tankard of beer on the table. We all sat down, passing the tankard around and filling our plates.

"I think we got all the ewes in the barn," Pa announced. "We'll have to be sure to keep the barn doors closed until they've all birthed. If wolves get in there, we'll have no wool, mutton or skins this year." We all nodded solemnly, understanding the importance of his warning.

"Cyrus, I'd like you to help me with the brewing this afternoon and Lucy too, if you can spare her, Orinda." Pa looked over at Ma, who nodded. I was pleased. Brewing was more fun than pooling and quilling. I wasn't yet big enough to spin and weave.

Ma commented, "Mr. Stacey wanted to stop by after supper and talk about his sermon." Abby turned red, and Becky giggled. Ma silenced her with a look. She turned to Abby. "Would you be able to make a fruit tart for Pa and Mr. Stacy and all of us, of course?"

"Yes, I'll do it before I do my weaving this afternoon." She ducked her head.

"All right. Lucy, Cyrus, come with me." Pa rose from the table. We obediently followed. I was glad I didn't have to clear things away. I'd rather do outdoor work.

We had gathered the Baldwin and Roxbury Russet apples last fall. We sweated them by storing them in large barrels to mellow. We put the barrels on wooden planks because the apples would rot if the barrels sat on the ground. Several months later, when Cyrus or I put an apple in our hands and squeezed it, it was all soft and kept our finger marks.

"I loaded some of the barrels with the mellowest apples onto the horse cart and brought them up here to the barn," Pa directed. "Lucy, you and Cyrus get a large tub pulled over here, and start filling it with water. Lucy, I want you to sort out the apples, throw the rotten ones in a pile, and we'll feed them to the pigs. When you have a bucket of those mellow apples sorted and ready, take the lot over to the hand-grinder in the corner, and Cyrus can crush the apples."

"Why can't I crush? Why does Cyrus get to do that?" I stamped my foot. I was older. Why did he get to do it?

Pa stopped, turned and spoke to me with a hint of irritation in his voice. "You're very careful, Sophronia. What your Ma calls a perfectionist. We need to be sure no rotten apples get in; otherwise the whole batch of cider could spoil. Cyrus is strong and can handle the crushing. Now I'm not going to have time to justify everything I ask you to do. Do you understand?"

I hung my head. I have real trouble being headstrong all the time. "Yes, Pa," I whispered.

Pa turned to Cyrus, "When you get a large bucket of ground apples, bring it over to me, and I'll press the grindings—we call it pomace—in that large wooden press over there. Do you both understand?" We nodded. Suddenly, we both felt important because generally the older girls did this, but they were busy helping Ma, so we set to work. And when I thought about it, I was secretly glad I got to sort the apples. I liked the soft feel when I pressed my fingers in and the fresh, sweet smell. The crunching machine made a little tune as the wheels turned.

After about an hour, Pa had enough pomace to start the presses, and a liquid Pa called "must" began to flow into the barrel placed under the press. We worked for another hour. Even though it was cold, bugs—attracted by the sweet smell—began to assemble.

"You two young'uns go in and get some gallon jugs. I'll start bottling some of the must now," Pa muttered

When we entered the cabin, we saw Ma sitting at the table talking to Mrs. Rath who had stopped by on her way back from town. We called Mrs. Rath "the Widder Croaker" since she could predict doom and death for even the most promising person or endeavor.

"Pa wants us to bring some cider jugs," we announced importantly.

"There's a sack on the hook back of the chimney. The clean jugs are on a shelf beside it," Ma pointed.

"I understand you're having morning sickness, Orinda." Widder Croaker looked at Ma over the cup in her hands. "When are you due?"

Cyrus went on piling jugs in the sack. I turned to watch.

Ma turned pale and through tight lips answered, "August."

"Oh, my, that's a bad month to be birthin'. All that heat generally affects either the ma or the newborn." Widder Croaker smiled smugly and took a sip of tea.

Minerva, who had been weaving stopped her loom and spoke into the strange silence, "Isn't that the month your grandson Harris was born? I remember you made him a cake, and he was so proud,"

Now we all knew Harris was the apple of her eye. A nice young man we all liked, strong as an ox, but slow when it came to schooling. He had a crush on Minerva, which was a pity, seeing as how she was the brightest student our school ever had.

"Well, I'd best be on my way." The Widder stood up and through narrowed eyes glared at Minerva who was innocently weaving again.

Ma walked her to the door, trying to keep her lips straight. Minerva was smiling sweetly. As soon as the Widder left, both Ma and Minerva started to laugh.

"What's so funny and when are you going to help me with these jugs?" Cyrus grumbled. I went over and held the sack for him. When it was full, we both carried it out to Pa. "Over here," Pa called and gestured at a large pot filled with water that had come to a boil. "Put the bottles in there. We'll boil 'em for about an hour and next we fill 'em with the must. In a few days the juice will ferment a little and we'll have some good sweet cider. In another week or so, when the fermenting stops, we'll have hard cider. Now, come into the shed and we'll start on this week's beer."

I loved the yeasty smell of the brewing shed even more than the aroma of the cider pots. It reminded me of fresh bread. The farmers always brewed beer on Saturdays, and we all drank it. Ma reconed it was weaker than hard cider. The water we drank sometimes made us sick. I don't know why, but if we cleaned all of the bottles with care, beer never did.

Becky and Pa already had chopped and pounded corn stalks and put them in a big copper kettle, where they had been simmering for hours. "Now," Pa cautioned, "you two stand back while I pour this wort though a strainer into that pot over there. Cyrus, take that long-handled shovel and steady the pot so it doesn't squirm away. Lucy, you help him, but stand way back from the handle." We held the shovel steady. Wearing leather gloves, Pa tipped the kettle, and the wort slowly began pouring through the wire sieve into the lower pot. When it had been transferred, Pa added hops and spruce tips and branches. "This spruce beer keeps us from getting scurvy."

"Why is that Pa?" I asked.

"I don't rightly know. Maybe someday, you'll figure it out." He smiled as he fastened a siphon to the fermenting barrel. "Now, while we let that boil, we can see about draining off last weeks' wort from the fermenting barrel." Pa was a big man, and that was good since those barrels weighed a ton! We held the large bottles that Becky already had washed and boiled clean under the siphon. Pa drew the liquid off the lees but didn't fill the bottles all the way up. As he capped them and placed them on the shelf, Pa chuckled, "We don't want those bottles too full or the gas will explode. we'd have a pretty mess."

After we filled all the bottles, Pa scooped the lees that had the yeast into tarred bottles and capped them. Ma would use some of that yeast for bread, and Pa would add the rest to the next batch of beer. "I'm going back to the beer shed," Pa told us as he moved toward the door. "That second pot should be cool enough to take the yeast. You two scrub out this barrel and light a sulphur candle in it to be sure it's clean. After you put those tarred bottles with the yeast in the root cellar to keep them cool, come in and help me get this brew in the fermenter after the foam dies down."

Once we had cleaned the barrel and trudged back and forth to the cellar with the bottles, we started up the stairs toward the beer shed. I don't know why, but I looked back to where the bottles of beer were stacked. A half bottle of wine that our Marlborough, Massachusetts, cousins had brought when they came to visit was sitting on the shelf. Although the grown-ups each had enjoyed a thimbleful, Ma had told Pa, after the company left, she didn't want it in the house. I never had tasted wine, and couldn't help but wonder why everybody made such a fuss about it.

"Cyrus, do you think we could just try a little of that wine?" I asked. "We have a few minutes before we have to go back"

Cyrus looked at me with wide, scared eyes. Something like daring took over. "Why not?" he cried.

I lifted the bottle down, found two tasting cups on the shelf and poured us each some. Feeling terribly wicked and afraid we'd be caught if we waited, we drank it down right away. Yuk! Both of us started to cough. Pa walked in.

We put the cups behind our backs, but Cyrus still held the bottle in his right hand. "Was this your idea?" He looked at Cyrus.

"No, Pa, I thought of it." I stood with my head down.

"Well, if you want to try it, I think you should finish the bottle. There's not much left. Your Ma would be glad to get it all gone. Hold out your cups." Pa filled them to the brim. We didn't dare say no. So both Cyrus and I drank that awful stuff. Our throats burned and our eyes watered. I peeked a glance at Pa. I swear he was grinning ear to ear. "Glad to get rid of that rotgut! Now we'll hear no more of this, unless you think you might want some more?"

"No, Pa, never!" I croaked. My throat was on fire. I felt dizzy.

"Come on back to the shed. We'll pour that yeast wort into the barrel." As we went outside, he stooped and picked some late-growing mint from the sheltered side of the basement. "Here, chew on this. It'll make your throat feel better and take away the smell. Maybe Ma won't get all worked up. That's all I need right now."

Pa acted like he didn't notice when Cyrus and I scooted to the side of the barn and threw up. We ran back, chewing that mint longer than old Betsy chewed her cud. Finally, when we had finished the last chore, we headed back to the kitchen for supper. I'll always hate wine and mint, I thought.

Supper went quickly because we were getting ready for Mr. Stacey's visit. I noticed Abby had put on the calico dress that she usually saved for church. Cotton was expensive, so we always wore linen clothes in the summer and wool in the winter from cloth we wove, but Ma and each of us girls had a calico dress for church.

We had just cleaned up the wooden chargers when Mr. Stacey arrived. He had on his Sunday suit but wore the same old patched boots I knew so well. They probably were the only ones he had.

He smiled all around and took the seat Pa offered by the fire. "Since I'm newly come to town," Mr. Stacey began, "I appreciate your consulting with me on this sermon, Peter, as I'm going to talk about God giving us land to grow our food. I thought I'd mention how the folks who live in these parts came here, when they arrived and how many stayed and settled into the community."

Becky giggled. "Any of your students could tell you that as well as Pa.".

Ma looked hard at her and spoke sternly, "Perhaps Mr. Stacey wanted to ask an older person who knew some of the early settlers and stories and didn't make statements to get attention. Becky, would you please put Eva to bed? It's way past her bedtime."

Red-faced, Becky trounced off in a huff pulling little Eva by the hand.

Pa turned to Mr. Stacey. "Well, now, let's see. The first settlement of Poultney was in 1771, when Ebenezer Allen and Thomas Ashley came here. Allen built a house for his family, who came with him. Ashley built a house, but his family came later. It was a busy time, clearing the land and trying to be ready for the Brits if they came. My family came from Massachusetts. They were always migrating, scouting out new and fertile land, just like the folks who are now going to the Ohio Territory in spite of the Indian threat and wild animals and floods. I think exploring is in my blood" He shot a look at Ma. For the first time it began to sink in for me that a journey to Ohio was dangerous, even fatal. In spite of the fire, I felt a chill. Pa continued,. "My Pa, Nehemiah Howe, built the first gristmill in Poultney up on the falls. At that time, men carried up to a hundred pounds of grain on their backs to the mill at Manchester, thirty miles away.

"When my uncle, Samuel Howe, was elected Moderator at a town meeting in 1772, they decided to build some roads. And my Pa and John Grant gave over some land for a burial place. That was a hard time. Everybody lived in rude log cabins, raised a little corn and kept one cow. Those men were strong, bold and determined but poor. In addition to clearing land where no white man had been, building a home and raising a family, those men had to deal with the New York claimants who were always demanding taxes. This wasn't a terribly religious community. Now the Allen brothers, talk about wild . . ."

Ma broke in, "Perhaps you'd like a piece of fruit tart that Abby baked today?" We had all been waiting for the tart. The warmth of the fire, the hard work and the wine, not to mention Pa's long-winded history, made Cyrus and me sleepy, but the promise of a tart had kept us awake. Two desserts in two days must be what heaven is like.

"My, oh, my, but this is good," Mr. Stacey broke forth in hearty praise. Abby blushed.

Becky, who had put Eva to bed and returned to the hearth, chided, "Oh, Abby is a good cook. Which is handy, since she likes to eat so much."

Abby turned to Mr. Stacey. "We are all very grateful for your quick thought and action in keeping the schoolhouse from burning down. Cyrus told us of Lucy's wild sleigh ride. Had you not acted at once, we might have lost the building and, worse, some of the children."

Mr. Stacey turned red with sheer pleasure all the way up to his receding hairline. I expect no one ever had praised him before . . . and for good reason!

"I take my charge very seriously, as I do anything I propose," he intoned and looked meaningfully at Abby. "I think Sophronia has a lively nature and sometimes gets into scrapes. But we all did as young'uns."

My head went up. That was the second time he'd called me Sophronia. And if the Reverend Mr. Matthew Stacey felt ever so understanding, why did he have me crunched up under his table all afternoon. I should have bitten his leg while I was under there.

Ma halted the sentence I was putting together in my head. "Lucy, you and Cyrus had better say good night. It's past your bedtime."

We dutifully mumbled "good night" and headed for the ladder to the loft. "Cyrus," I whispered, "I'm sorry I got you in trouble with the wine. I'm not going to pinch you any more going up the ladder. At least, I'll try not to."

CHAPTER FOUR

RESCUING A LADY

S ap begins to move in the trees when the nights are still below freezing but the days get above 50 degrees. Several weeks ago when the temperature was exactly right, Pa went out to the grove of maples to tap the trees and we went with him. Choosing only those trees that were ten inches in diameter or bigger, he moved from one maple to the next, drilling holes in sound wood about two inches deep and anywhere from two to four feet above the ground. We would stick our fingers in the hole to see if there was any sap. Pa would shout, "Fingers out of the way!"

The sap tasted watery and had little bits of wood from the drilling in it. As soon as he made each hole, he wanted to insert a collection spout and tap it into the tree. He placed as many as three taps in some of the bigger trees. We followed him lugging buckets that made a clanging noise and hung buckets under the spouts. Sarah covered the buckets to keep out rainwater, insects and loose bits of dirt and bark falling from the trees. When the buckets were full, we started gathering them and dumped the thin sap into big copper kettles. The sap simmers a long time before it begins to thicken as the water evaporates. The heat from the kettles is awful. All of our kettles were protected under a makeshift roof. I like the sweet smell all around as the sap boils down. The sweet smell stays in our hair and clothes. It takes a lot of sap, about thirty-five to forty-five gallons, to make one gallon of maple syrup. We have kept the fires burning night and day, and someone watched them all the time. Making maple syrup was my favorite chore.

"Ready or not, here I come!" Sarah yelled. She had forgotten that she was thirteen years old as she played hide and seek with us younger children. She lost her shyness and as she ran and waved her arms over her head, her brown pigtails flew out behind her and her apron blew up in her face. We were in among the maple trees. The low-growing shrubbery gave excellent cover for hiding. We were supposed to be gathering the drain buckets from the maple trees and carrying them to the boiling kettle, but the cool air of early spring called out to us to play.

I heard Sarah calling "ready or not" as I ducked behind a little sumac bush close to the trail coming from the house. "I see you," Sarah called as she spied Cyrus and ran back to the maple tree to tag him out.

"Not fair!" Cyrus cried, his face red. "You were peeking. I saw you."

I looked over my shoulder and saw Ma walking up the path from the house. I jumped out of my hiding place and called in a loud whisper, "Quick, here comes Ma!" Everyone immediately ran out of hiding. When Ma got to the pots of boiling sap, three of us were busily checking the buckets under the taps. Sarah was stirring the pot.

"Ma, do you feel well enough to be out?" I was still worried about her, how white she was—and so thin.

"I'm fine, Lucy. I just had to get out of the house and get some fresh air. Something about early spring starts my yearning for the outdoors. But I do tire easily, so I'll just plunk down here for a minute and catch my breath. Sarah, I'm proud of you for doing the stirring and watching the fire under the kettle. Generally an older girl does that. We have to keep a close eye on that heat and skim off any crusty scum. You young'uns have been so busy. Why don't you take a rest too?" We looked at each other guiltily and went to sit beside her.

Ma pulled her shawl closer around her shoulders and smiled, "Have you ever heard the story the Indians tell about maple syrup?" We were a little at a loss. Ma never took time off in a busy morning and certainly not to tell stories. That was really unusual, but we all loved storytelling and quickly drew closer. "Well," she continued, "there are many versions, so I'll tell you my favorite. Once upon a time, there was a young chief named Glooskap."

"Glooskap?" We all shrieked with delight. "Really was that his name?"

Mother nodded. "Yes. He had magic powers. He could fly like an eagle high above the earth. Now, in the beginning, maple trees were full up with maple syrup, not sap. All the Indians would just lie around a tap hole and drink syrup. Even the dogs and cats would find a place to lap it up. Glooskap was a worker, a good worker. When he saw everyone doing nothing, he thought: *This will never do. Who will build fires at night to keep us warm? Or get skins for cloths? Or tend our horses?* So he made a big bowl out of bark, flew to a nearby river, filled the bark bowl with water and flew back, dumping the water on the trees. It so diluted the syrup that it became sap. He ordered, 'You must boil the sap to get syrup. The sap will only run in the early spring, so you had best be quick!'"

"No wonder he was called Glooskap. That was a pretty stupid thing to do. I think the Indians should have shot him!" Cyrus stood up.

Mother smiled. "Well, however it happened, we have to boil sap so you'd best be getting back to it."

Still angry at being tagged first and in a foul mood, Cyrus took the bucket of sap he had in his hand and threw it in the kettle. Some of the boiling sap splashed on his hand and, when he jumped, he lost his footing and fell against the boiling kettle. He started to scream and dance about. Ma jumped to her feet and dragged him over to a pile of snow that hadn't melted yet. "Quick, cover all his burned places with snow!" she commanded. We all scurried around piling snow on the squirming, yelling Cyrus until he looked like a snowman. Gradually he stopped screaming. Through his burnt clothes, we saw large red welts on his back, hand and arm beginning to blister, so we kept piling on the snow.

"I think you can stop now." Ma sat down hard, her face ashen. "Let me catch my breath a bit. Lucy, run and fetch your Pa. Ask him to come and see that Cyrus gets to the cabin, where I can put some lard on his burns.

I ran to the barn as fast as I could. "Hurry, Pa, Ma wants you to come fast. Cyrus got mad and threw his bucket of syrup in the kettle. It spilt out, and he has burnt himself badly. Ma looks as pale as a ghost!" He ran beside me as I gulped out all that had happened. Pa looked more worried about Ma than about Cyrus when he got to the kettle.

He hurriedly took Ma's arm, staring at her hard. "Are you all right, Orinda?" She nodded quietly and seemed embarrassed. With the other hand, Pa got hold of Cyrus's arm that wasn't burned and roughly swung him over his shoulder. Supporting Ma, he headed back to the cabin at a quick pace. "After you three finish emptying the buckets, come on back," he called over his shoulder. "And do it carefully!"

In a sober mood, and with great care, we emptied each bucket into the kettle. Sarah watched us closely as she stirred the pot. "In another few days, the sap flow will be over. We can bottle this when enough water has evaporated," she whispered mostly to herself in a comforting way. When the last bucket was emptied, Sarah covered the kettle loosely and turned to us. "Let's go see how Cyrus is doing."

"Can you leave the kettle, Sarah?" I didn't want any more upsets.

"I'll come right back and watch the kettle and stir," she murmured. Clearly, Sarah was worried.

Cyrus was lying on a pile of quilts that Abby had fashioned into a pallet by the fire. His burns had been greased and wrapped in linen bandages. Obviously enjoying the attention, Cyrus groaned every once in a while. Mother was seated in a rocker knitting. "Cyrus," she advised quietly, "I think you should sleep down here by the fire tonight so I can keep an eye on you. Becky, I'd like you to take charge of the maple kettle. Lucy, after noon meal, you and Sarah help Pa in the smoke shed with the pork."

I felt like groaning. I dreaded that chore. We butchered pork in November and salted it down good. In early spring we washed off the extra salt, covered the meat with pepper and hung it in the smoke house. I wished I could go back to the maple trees, but I followed Sarah to the smoke shed instead. Pa had lifted the meat that was salted and dried over to the washtubs for us to scrub off the salt. I hated that job because, when you wash off the salt, your hands get all dried out, red and cracked. The pepper made me sneeze and the hickory smoke from the fire Pa had started and dampened made my eyes water. I had black thoughts of Cyrus lying all comfy in a bed by the fire.

Sarah was a good worker and serious. I never had thought of her as being fun. Yet when Pa went out to get some more wood, she whispered, "Lucy, look!" She picked up a big ham and started dancing around the room with the ham as a partner. Sarah was small for her age but agile. When she smiled a dimple popped in on her left cheek. She kicked up her heels and her apron swirled over the ham.

I started to laugh and, grabbing a ham, danced over to her drawling, "I think my partner has the most muscle but needs a mustache." We played as if we were in a square dance doing do-si-dos. Luckily we heard Pa coming back and were busy scrubbing when he came in.

When the last piece of pork was scraped, washed, peppered and hung to smoke, we went back to the house. Abby and Becky were dressing one of the looms that Pa had made. Abby was precise and accurate so she carefully measured lengths of yarn on a board with a series of pegs. Becky attached each of the strands of yarn lengthwise from the back beam to the cloth beam stick at the front of the loom. She gave each strand an extra tug 'cause she was angry. Becky also wound yarn around a bobbin that could be threaded back and forth through the lengthwise strands to produce an interlocking weave Becky hated busy work.

Minerva was busy spinning. Everyone else was tiptoeing around so as not to wake Cyrus. I was ready to go over, give him a big shove and tell him to get back to work! Ma must have read my thoughts. "Lucy, let's help Abby and Becky now. Would you please card some flax? Sarah you can spool and warp now."

Large bundles of linen yarn decorated our kitchen walls in the spring and were replaced in summer with woolen yarn. We raised our own flax. We harvested it in August and spread it out on the ground to dry. Becky always got mad when we had to bundle it up until harvest was done, spread it out on the ground again and let the sun and rain rot the stalks until they were brittle. "Someone should find a way to just leave flax on the ground. Talk about extra work!"

Pa and some of his friends broke, and swingled the flax. Sweat ran down their faces. It was heavy work. Ma and the older girls hatched the flax, separating the tow from the flax or fibrous parts. They wound the flax on the distaff of the little wheel, and the tow was carded and spun on the large wheel.

Above the whoosh of the looms and the hum of the spinning wheel, I could hear Becky ask, "So what did Mr. Stacy have to say after I left? Did he ever get around to proposing? I thought he was going to eat you up the way he looked at you."

Abby was blushing. "He said he hoped to see me in church tomorrow."

"That's all? Honestly, you can do better than that old stud. You're pretty and smart, even if you do eat like a horse and will probably end up fat. If I couldn't do better than that, I'd do without!" Becky boasted and shook her head for emphasis.

"I guess that explains why you don't have a gentleman friend, Becky," Minerva commented quietly from the corner where she was spinning.

"Well, Miss Smarty Pants, that clod Harris Rath is certainly no catch." Becky blurted, working the foot pedals of the loom faster and faster as her cheeks flushed. "Anyway, there is no one around here I'd care to have!"

Nothing ever seemed to rile Minerva. "Whoever marries Harris will have a hardworking, honest, gentle husband. Harris and I are good friends because, when he has a hard time at school, I'm the only one who doesn't make fun of him in the cruel way some folks have."

Always the ringleader in making fun of people, Becky knew Minerva's comment was meant for her. She tossed her head and changed the subject. "Submit Brown's cousin from Philadelphia is visiting the Browns. She's been sickly and her folks want her to be away from Philadelphia 'cause there's a lot of pleurisy going around. This cousin has told Submit about the big houses in town. The ladies all wear fancy clothes—calico for everyday and silk on Sunday. She confided that the Southern Colonies are even finer and richer. Did you know George Washington owns thousands of acres in Virginia?"

That was impressive. We owned one hundred acres, but we had never felt poor. Uncle Silas had the gristmill from Grandpa and had built a sawmill, but that seemed nothing in comparison. Becky continued, pleased that she had silenced us all. "I'm going to marry one of those rich Southerners. I don't blame Squire Prouty for wanting to go to Ohio, where you can get lots of land cheaply."

"Let's see, you think you're going to meet some rich Southerner in Ohio?" Minerva gave a little shrug. "Geography never was your best subject, Becky."

For some reason, I had never thought about the person I would marry. I had lots of friends, but getting married was for old folks. I had begun to think, though, about growing older like Abby had. The new thought made me feel sick at the stomach.

Ma came over to the looms. "I think we'd best get ready for supper, girls." We all left our places and started the nightly chores. I wondered what those rich Southerners were eating at night.

Cyrus seemed to be having more pain. I noticed that some of the blisters looked red, and pus was forming. After supper, Ma called

Abby aside. "I'm going to need some help. Those blisters look bad. We'll need to clean them out. Get Minerva to bring hot water and lye soap. I want you girls to hold him while I do it."

She sat down beside Cyrus with the basin of water and some of our strong lye soap, and started to work. Abby and Minerva held him on each side as he screamed and struggled. Very quietly Ma proceeded to lance and bathe each of the blisters with hot water and soap.

I couldn't watch. I went up the ladder and hid in my bed. I could hear Cyrus screaming and moaning and covered my ears with a feather pillow. Finally, it grew quiet, and I crept back downstairs. Cyrus was sleeping, completely worn out. Already having cleaned the basin and replaced the soiled quilts, Abby was washing the floor around him.

Ma and Pa sat by the fire. Pa saw me and told me, "Come here, Lucy. Your brother's going to be all right now. We just couldn't let that infection go on. He might have lost his arm. Cyrus has a temper, and I hope he's learned from this that he has to control it, or he can get in a whale of a lot worse trouble than some burns. I'll try to take him with me more and build up his confidence. Lucy, you can help. Much as he taunts you, I think he really is respectful of you."

I thought about what Pa suggested, and there and then I decided to do all I could to help Cyrus . . . even if he was a toad. "What can I do?"

Pa patted my hand. "You're a smart girl, Lucy. I know you'll find a way to make him feel good about himself."

As the weather got warmer and the trees began to bud, the sap would no longer be good for making syrup. So in the next few days, we finished emptying the sap buckets. As soon as the syrup was cooler, Sarah and I siphoned it off through woolen filters into the clean bottles and jugs we'd taken up to the maple grove. We put part of the thick syrup from the bottom of the kettles into cone-shaped clay pottery bowls with fine drainage holes. As the water drained off through these holes, brown sugar formed in cone shapes. Most of the scrapings we poured on tin plates and had cakes of brown sugar when they dried out. We scooped up the parts that crumbled and licked our fingers and tasted sweet, crunchy, yummy sugar. We seldom had white sugar. It was too expensive.

The following week the spring rains began. Cyrus was getting much better and was able to go out a little. One evening, just before dark a heavy rain set in, Cyrus called, "Lucy, have you seen Lady? I've looked all over for her today and couldn't find her. Would you try?"

Lady was a dog that had wandered onto the farm and become attached to Cyrus and he to her. The dog with the dignified name of Lady was a mongrel—part sheep dog, part wolf, part heavens-knows-what. But the dog was big and gave good protection to the sheep, so Pa had kept her. I looked outside at the pouring rain and at Cyrus's face. "All right," I grunted. I have never had a love of dogs or cats. I guess that's because it always had fallen to me to take care of them if they were hurt or hungry or needed to have ticks removed.

I put a tarpaulin over my head, slipped into Ma's boots, which were way too big for me, and started out sloshing around the barnyard. It was barely light, but my eyes soon grew used to the dark. Over in a ravine behind the barn, I thought I heard whining. I crept to the edge. Down at the foot of the ravine were lady and six new pups.

What a mess! My first problem was how to get down into the ravine to save her. The next was how to get out again. I saw a rock pile at the other end of the slope. The rocks looked loose and slick. Moss was growing over some, a perfect place for snakes to hide. With slippery footing, I made my way over to it and crept down beside the dogs. The water had made a floor of slushy mud. The pups were wet and cold. I picked three up in my hands and started to struggle up the slick rocks. With much sliding I made it to the barn. I did my best to make a nest out of some straw and deposited the little fellows in it, I went back for the next three. It was getting really dark. I could see big bolts of lightning in the distance. Slick mud covered everything and I crawled back down on my knees, gathered up the last three pups and made my slow way back to the barn. The first little pups seemed dry and were mewing and squeaking for food. I set my little charges down beside the first three and trudged back to the ravine, which was filling up with water. The lightning was getting closer and the thunder came in deafening claps. I shuddered from cold rain running down my neck

When I got back down next to Lady, I realized, for the first time, how big she was. I tried to lift her, but she was just dead weight. I guessed she was worn out with the birthing. So I stooped

over, wrapped her paws over my upper arm and lifted her onto my shoulders. I looked down. The water was way up above my knees, past the top of Ma's boots, and my feet kept sloshing around inside. I had a hard time on the rocks and slipped once almost all the way back down. After what seemed like hours, I reached the welcome shelter of the barn and deposited a bedraggled Lady beside her pups. I got some dry gunnysacks from a rack by the barn door and tried to dry Lady off. The newborn pups were nosing around trying to find her teats and nurse. Five of them made it, but one little fellow, smaller than the rest, just couldn't hold his own. So I scooped him up and started to run for the house. All at once, a blazing flash of lightning struck about fifty yards away from me followed immediately by a loud clap of thunder. I screamed and ran like mad all the way to the kitchen door.

"Lucy, where in the world were you? We were frantic! You know you shouldn't go out in a lightning storm!" Standing just inside the door, Ma sounded really angry, her voice sharp. "We were going out to look, but I couldn't find my boots!"

"I borrowed them," I sniffed. "Cyrus asked me to find Lady, and I did. She was in the ravine behind the barn. She'd given birth to six pups. The ravine was filling with water, so I thought I'd best get them out quick. I did. I got them all to the barn. Lady, too." I was shaking I was so cold.

"Honey, Lady is a big dog. How did you do it?" Pa bent over to remove the tarpaulin.

"I did what you did with Cyrus when you brought him home. I put her over my shoulders. This little fellow wasn't able to nurse. Can we feed him?"

Ma looked steadily at me all quiet for a moment, not mad at all now. She hugged me, gently pinched my cheek. Turning she reached for the little pup. "Abby, heat some milk. Lucy, take off those boots and your wet cloths. You'll catch your death. Becky, bring some dry things."

Cyrus came over and stood in front of me. Very softly, softer than I had ever heard him speak, he whispered, "Thank you, Lucy.

Lady means a lot to me. She would have died and so would the pups."

I had never noticed how blue his eyes were. He seemed very serious. Probably the most serious I'd ever seen him, no teasing or acting brave.

"Sure, Cyrus, I know Lady is important to you. That's why I did it." I was surprised to hear myself add, "You're important to us," but I knew it was the truth.

"Look at this little fellow eat." Ma had dipped a small piece of linen into the warm milk. Once it was sopping wet, she held it near the puppy's nose to let drops of milk fall to his tongue. "He'll be able to take his place in the barn with the others in a couple of days."

"Well done, Lucy. Well done." Pa patted me on the head.

I sloshed up the ladder. Abby helped me into dry clothes and gave me a big hug. "I'm proud of you, Lucy. That took a lot of courage and you were smart to get them to the barn." She hugged me again. That night I slept like a baby with no fears of Ohio.

CHAPTER FIVE

A POISONOUS PERIL
IN THE BLACKBERRY PATCH

B y the middle of May, we were out of school and glad to be working outdoors. Throughout the spring we'd been busy planting our crops. Cyrus's arm and back were healed, but he would carry some scars for the rest of his life. Thomas and I spent many sunny spring days sowing the aboveground grains and setting out plants during the phase of the lunar cycle known as "the light of the moon," when there was a full or nearly full moon. On those days that fell during "the dark of the moon," when there was only a sliver of the moon in the night sky, we worked from early morning through the heat of the day putting the bulbs and root vegetables in the ground. I asked Pa, "Why do we do plant according to the phases of the moon?"

"I don't rightly know, Lucy. We've always done it, and things seem to grow if there is rain and sun, so I've never questioned it." He looked perplexed. Ma asked him to bring in more wood. I think he forgot my question. One day I got some onion bulbs and, on my own, planted them in the ground in "the light of the moon." They seemed to be doing as well as those planted when the moon was in its darker crescent stage. I never told Pa, he'd think I took a chance wasting perfectly good onion bulbs.

After the crops were in, Pa started making bricks. We helped him. "We can sell the bricks we don't use to the town for the new school building they plan to put up. Lucy, you like to try new things. Come and see what I'm building." I followed him out to the brickyard and, of course, so did Cyrus, Thomas and even little Eva. Pa had a brick bed, which was a grass-free plot of ground about twenty feet in diameter with planks around the sides. He had put clay, sand and water in the bed. Usually Pa would drive oxen into the bed to have them stomp around, mixing the material into mortar. It was a long, hard job.

That morning Pa pointed out a post he'd just put in the middle of the bed. He showed us a board he had fixed up that was about ten feet long, broad on one end and tapered off at the other end and had cogs all along its length. A swivel on the post in the middle of the bed was attached to the tapered end. The broad end hung out over the planks of the bed and had a sturdy handle. Pa had hitched the oxen to the handle and was driving them around the outside of the bed.

"Pa that is so smart! It looks a lot easier and faster!" We were all impressed. "What do you call it?"

He laughed, "I call it a horry-co-morry to tread mortar." A new word was born. We rolled it over our tongues. "Now you all get busy. I've shaped some bricks and they're lying flat on the ground. You can edge those and hake the dry ones."

We scrambled over to the bricks that were partially dry. We edged them by turning them up on their sides to help them dry better. Next we piled the bricks that were completely dry in long rows called hakes. That took all afternoon.

"After supper, come to the shanty where I am burning bricks," Pa called. "When I get enough, I'll make a kiln." It took a week to burn the bricks, and Pa kept the fires going night and day. We ate quickly and did our chores so we could go and watch the fires burning in the arches. Ma told us we could stay until bedtime.

The early summer nights were cool, but the little shanty was warm and cozy. The flames of the blazing fire hypnotized us. Minerva, who had come with us, pointed to a little spider weaving a web in the corner. "See that? I am the namesake of the one who made her!"

"What are you talking about?" Sarah asked.

"Didn't I ever tell you that story?" Minerva asked, shifting to a more comfortable position. We all loved stories and spent many nights making them up and telling them to each other. That and going to meeting or visiting neighbors was most of our entertainment. Minerva was a wonderful storyteller, and, as I mentioned, was the smartest of all of us at schooling. She told me that she wanted to be a teacher. I'd never heard of a woman teacher, but she could do it. Her math was better than Pa's. And right now, she could correct Mr. Stacey in grammar and spelling, though she never did.

"The teacher before Mr. Stacey let me read a book about old civilizations in Rome and Greece," she began. Minerva sat very straight. She was taller than most girls and very thin. Her brown eyes sparkled as if she was going to tell a tall tale. The fire made her dark brown hair look almost black. "My name is that of the Roman goddess Minerva. In Greece the same goddess was named Athena." We all caught our breath, very impressed.

"In the story," she continued, "Minerva wasn't born like other folk. She sprang full-grown from the head of Jupiter. She was the goddess of learning, agriculture, spinning and weaving. She also was the goddess of war, but defensive war, not the violent kind that the god Mars liked.

"Well, one day, a young woman named Arachne was told that she was the greatest weaver in all the world. She became so conceited that when someone suggested the Goddess Minerva must have taught her, Arachne got on her high horse and taunted, 'I'm better than Minerva!'"

We were all spellbound. How wonderful to be named for an ancient Roman goddess! Our sister continued, "The goddess Minerva, in the disguise of an old woman, went to Arachne and told her to ask the goddess's pardon. But that conceited girl refused." We all gasped. "So they had a contest. Minerva wove a beautiful cloth, but Arachne wove a cloth that was judged finer than Minerva's. The goddess got so mad that she stormed, 'You will spend all eternity spinning!' She sprinkled some old Roman juices over her. Arachne's hair, nose and ears came off. Except for a round belly, she got smaller and smaller until poof . . . she turned into a spider . . . and continued to spin, just as the goddess Minerva predicted she would!"

"Oh! That's the best story yet. Tell it again," we all pleaded.

"No. It's time for bed, but maybe tomorrow night." Minerva herded us all back to the house. In bed that night I wondered if there was a Roman goddess named Lucy. Probably not.

Spring cleaning began next day. Ma called up. "Do the beds first!" Abby and Minerva pulled the tickings outside and emptied out the old straw. The wind blew it around and we all sneezed. Sarah and I put in fresh, clean-smelling new straw. Sarah giggled 'cause we looked like scare crows with all the straw in our hair and over our dresses.

"We always do this after threshing. Why did Ma want it done early this year?" I asked as I spit out a straw that was stuck on my lips.

Abby and Minerva exchanged looks. "That's for her to know and you to guess." Abby answered rather crossly. "Now you and Sarah take those ticks over to Becky so she can sew the ticking back up again."

Each bed had knobs down both of the side rails and across the head and foot rails, too. Abby and Minerva stretched ropes cross ways and wrapped around the knobs starting at the headboard and back and forth on the side rails to make a lattice to support the tickings. Pa had made the ropes out of the same sisal fiber he'd used to make the seats of our chairs.

"Now the fun part!" Becky yelled. We all jumped on the beds and bounced up and down to check the bed ropes to be sure they were still strong. "Keep it down," Abby called out, "or Ma will hear and we'll have no supper!" When we were all tired out, we giggled as we tumbled out of the beds and unsrung the ropes. Abby was in control again. "Now, everyone pick up these ropes, take them outside and put them in the pots of boiling water. When they're dry, we'll restring the beds."

That afternoon we started on the pillows. We all took them out to air. Sarah and I beat them with wire beaters to get out the dust. Cyrus helped. "Take that!" Cyrus shouted as he hit one pillow so hard the string holding it shut burst. He looked worried.

Abby must have felt sorry for him. She came over and whispered, "Put it over on that pile with the flat pillows. We have to open them and add some of the feathers we've been saving each time we killed chickens for dinner. But I warn you, don't hit that hard again!"

While we worked on the bedding, Pa had been plowing. I looked out to the field. He was leaning on the plow talking to three of our neighbors. They seemed real excited. When I looked to the house, I saw Ma had been hanging out the wash, but she was watching the men too. I recognized them: Mr. Hopson, Mr. Putnam and Mr. Prindle. Mr. Hopson and his wife, Laura, had three children and owned about sixty acres out east of town. Mr. Putnam had two children. His wife, Clara, was one of those people who complained about everything. Mr. Prindle was just married. He and his wife, Jessie, had taken up forty acres not far from us. Cyrus and my sisters saw me staring and turned to look too.

Ma called out, "If you've got nothing better to do than gawk at your Pa, you'd best get on with the soap making."

Cyrus cringed. He still remembered the cleaning his blistered arm and back had got. We started with a large barrel that had a spout hanging down from the hole in the bottom and a container under the spout. Cyrus put straw down in the bottom of the barrel and filled it with hickory ashes from the fireplace. The straw kept the ashes from dropping through the spout. I poured water—a gallon or two at a time—into the barrel. Gradually lye, a caustic brownish-colored liquid, came out of the spout. We collected the lye in a bucket and boiled it in a large kettle with ten to fifteen pounds of leftover suet, lard from the fall hog butchering and grease left from cooking. Every time we emptied the lye into the fat, Cyrus gagged. The liquid got thick as it boiled.

"I've stirred it enough! Cyrus, it's your turn." I called out.

"Lucy, could you do it for me? I'll do any of your chores for you, honest. I just hate the smell of that lye soap. It makes me sick ever since those burns." Cyrus was turning pale.

I was ready to shout no, when I remembered what Pa had said. "All right, if you'll feed the hogs and water the horses." Nothing like driving a hard bargain—two chores for one!

Cyrus must have been serious because he agreed right away and took off. I felt very virtuous, very clever and also very relieved. I always got so tired working the pump for the horses' watering log. Pa had scooped out a log three feet in diameter and about six feet long. It took a long time to pump enough water to fill it up.

We made fifty pounds of soap that day and it's a good thing because we used it doing all our laundry and on dirty pots and pans and everything else Ma thought needed cleaning. The new batch of soap was getting thicker and thicker. Some folk used it like that—as a thick liquid. But Ma wanted her soap in bars, so I put in cornhusks to thicken the brew some more. I cooked it longer to get rid of more water, and scooped the thick soapy liquid out into wooden boxes. After it cooled and dried out, I would cut it into bars. My hands were always red from the strong lye in the soap.

After our noon meal, Sarah and I went out to the blackberry patch to collect berries for jam and jelly. Some of our neighbors made blackberry wine, but Ma decided we had enough beer and cider to drink, and she wanted jelly.

The sun was hot on our backs. We ate one berry for every ten we picked. Our lips and tongues were soon dark blue. "We'd best stop eating or we'll not get enough for jelly, and Ma will be mad," Sarah cautioned.

My back ached from stooping, and my fingers were covered with scratches from the thorns of the bushes. We had been picking and following the line of the bushes as they grew down towards the little stream that wandered over our property. From the berry patches and the fields, the stream ran near the house. Part of the stream was diverted to flow over the floor of the milk house where we kept our milk, cream and butter to cool. "Sarah, let's take a break. Just for a few minutes. No one can see us from the house. We can run our hands in the stream and get some of this color off." I stared down the bank.

"Don't fall in!" Sarah called.

I stopped near a sandy bog and swished my hands in the water. A piece of bark was near my right hand. I scooped it up. "Look, Sarah. A ship! Let's see if we can get it to float downstream." I found a twig nearby, fastened a large oak leaf to it for a sail and stuck the twig onto the bark with some wet clay. "Here she goes!"

The proud little ship traveled about ten feet and struck an outcropping of twigs and sank "Let's see if we can do another." I went further up the bank and got some more bark. Soon Sarah and I had a whole fleet ready to set sail. We jumped up and down as the fleet filled the stream, and some of the mighty ships made it around the bend.

Satisfied with our success, I looked up at Sarah and immediately froze. Not ten feet from her was a large coiled snake lying in the sun by the water. "Sarah, don't move. Don't run or anything. Just do exactly as I say. Very quietly start to back up the bank. Do it very slowly." I stooped down and reached for a thick oak branch lying on the ground. I could see the wide, dark crossbands on the snake's back. I should have known not to come to the banks of the stream. Snakes come out to water in the spring. Also, in the spring they usually move in pairs, so another one might be close by. I glanced around but didn't see anything, so I started to move up the bank too, keeping Sarah in view. When we got to the top of the bank, I shouted, "Now, run!"

Standing behind, the snake I lashed out and squashed it's head with the oak club. It lay motionless.

Sarah's eyes were huge. "What was it?"

"It was a snake. I think it was a timber rattler. It was about five feet long and yellowish-tan." I drew a deep breath. "That's a real deadly one!"

We were both shaking. Sarah turned to me after several minutes, "Lucy, I think we'd best not worry Ma with this. Let's finish the berries."

I nodded, and with great swiftness we finished picking the patch. It's funny how the thought of snakes can make you work so much faster.

We were both very quiet during dinner. Pa, who always could tell when something was bothering me, asked, "You feeling all right, Lucy?"

"Yes, Pa. I'm just tired." I avoided Sarah's eyes. She was staring at her plate, so I couldn't have connected with her if I'd wanted to.

That night I couldn't sleep. I just kept seeing that big old snake. Everyone else was soundly snoring when I crept to the opening over the ladder. I could see Ma and Pa sitting by the fire talking. So I listened.

"I saw you had some company out in the fields today," Ma offered and adjusted the knitting in her lap.

"Yep. Hopson, Putnam and Prindle stopped by." Ma waited. The silence lasted several minutes. She was bound not to ask why they had come. Finally, Pa confided, "It seems they've agreed to go to the far west of Ohio and want us to come too." I heard Ma suck in her breath.

"This is a hard decision to make, Orinda, but one we need to make together. Our baby's due in August. They plan to leave for Ohio September ninth. If the baby comes on time, it'll be only six weeks old. We're talking about a five-hundred-mile trip that'll take the best part of two-to-three months. I just don't know if you and the baby will be up to it. Plus I'll have to sell the farm and get us all packed up. I've put a lot of hard work into this place. It would be a wrench to leave. We have a lot of friends, and our families are here. We've just got the apple orchard to where it's bearing. The house, barn and outbuildings are all built up. And we've not had any Indian uprisings, so it's more-or-less safe. We'd also have to get wagons and cover them and probably do something about canoes if we use the river. I've pooh poohed it, but this is a dangerous journey. Some of the Indians are still hurting for how they've been treated and I can't say I blame 'em. That land out there is wild, bears, snakes, mountain lions. The rivers are treacherous and swifter than any we know. This is the Northwest Territory a vast unexplored area."

"You've told me why we shouldn't go, but, Peter, I feel you'd like to make the move anyway. What are the reasons you want us *to* go?" Ma had folded the knitting and put it in the basket so she could give Pa her full attention.

"Well, the soil here is poor and rocky," he began. "We've used up most of the forest mulch that was on the land when we cleared it, so we're going to have to start fertilizing or do something to keep up the yields. The winters here are dreadful cold, and Ohio is supposed to have a warmer climate."

Ma laughed. "Peter, just about any place on earth would have a warmer climate!"

"I'm not getting any younger, Orinda. If we're going to move, it should be soon. The land in Ohio is cheap—a lot cheaper than here. I've gone about as far as I can on this place. I don't have enough to buy any more land, what with the prices going up. And you've seen how the town of Poultney is growing."

Ma sat quietly a long time, thinking. I could hear the clock ticking. When she finally turned to Pa., I thought she was crying. I'd never seen Ma cry. "I've known this was coming for a long time," she admitted. "I've heard others talking about it, Squire Prouty for one." She made a face. "I could see you were restless. I can't concede I'm happy about moving. It means a lot of work. As for the baby and me, well, it's the pregnancy that's hard on me. I'm always stronger after a baby comes, so I'm not worried about that. Our babies always have been healthy. Mr. Hopson, Mr. Putnam and Mr. Prindle are good men and would make dependable travelers. Though I must admit I dread being on a two-month journey with Clara Putnam. You were thinking about putting up another house anyway, so this would be a good time to go. With prices rising, we could get a fair amount for this place. I guess what I'm saying is . . . yes. It isn't often that you have a chance to do something you really want to, Peter. I, too, think we should go."

Well, everything went quiet. When I peeked over the loft opening, Pa was holding Ma. I tried to be real quiet as I got back in bed. Sleep was out of the question. I felt a mixture of dread and excitement. I knew every foot of our land, the maple groves, the stream, even if it did have snakes, the house and the barn. I felt sad. Spring is always the prettiest time of the year. I thought about a covered wagon and maybe riding in a canoe. What fun! There might even be Indians! A whole new land to explore! One thing I was certain of, I mustn't let anyone know what I'd heard. Eavesdropping was considered a sin in our family. So I lay thinking until I heard the cock crow in the early morning light.

CHAPTER SIX

A Baby is Born

Early the next morning, after he had finished milking and feeding, Pa rode over to Squire Prouty and Eliza's house. I guessed he was going to talk with them about going to Ohio. I kept watching for Pa to return while I fed the chickens and helped carry in firewood. When at last he entered the kitchen, he just nodded to Ma. She looked relieved and smiled. All morning long I was fit to bust to tell someone. Finally after we all had finished our big noontime dinner, Pa, seated at the end of the table, spoke. "Your mother and I have decided to move our family to Ohio. I went over and talked to Ezra and Eliza this morning, and they are going too. Mr. Hopson, Mr. Putnam and Mr. Prindle and their families are leaving on September ninth. So I figure we'll make up about thirty people leaving from Poultney.

How amazing that one statement can change so many people's lives. After a stunned silence, everyone started talking at once. Becky was excited. "Well, good! Now we'll have a chance to meet some cultured, well-to-do people!"

Minerva laughed, "Yes, in the wilds of Ohio!"

Abby looked worriedly at Ma. "How do you feel about this?"

"We talked last night, and this is my decision too. I'll be fine." Ma seemed resolved. She patted Abby's hand.

"Whee! Indian country! What hunting! Do we get to see the Ohio River? I hear it's huge and fast! People drown in it all the time!" Cyrus's excitement got Thomas all worked up.

Sarah looked scared, so I leaned over and whispered, "If the Putnams are going, I guess William will be going, too." Sarah liked William Putnam even if she never dared make a squeak to him at school. She smiled.

Pa spoke into the excited melee, "There is going to be a lot of work this summer getting ready. We have the threshers coming to cut the grain before we leave. We'll all have to pitch in to get the corn harvested and have some of it ground. There's also the wheat and barley. We'll need to get everything sorted out and packed up. I'll have to get provisions and put the place up for sale. And Ma will supervise what we need to take in the way of household goods." Suddenly the room grew quiet as it dawned on each of us that we'd be leaving the only place we ever had known. The place we had called home all our lives. And the work sounded impossible. The rest of the day everyone carried on in a daze, swinging between feeling sad and feeling excited.

I was surprised how fast word of our leaving spread. Several ladies stopped in on their way to town to offer Ma best wishes or sympathy, depending on the nature of the visitor. That night, just after supper, we were surprised by a brief visit from Mr. Stacey. He hadn't taken time to put on his Sunday coat. He seemed embarrassed and fidgeted in his seat. After he had commented on the weather several times, he finally murmured to Pa, "I heard you're going west to Ohio, and I'd like to go too, if that's all right with you and the others."

Sitting quietly in the corner, Abby had been tense. She relaxed and turned pink.

Pa exclaimed, "We'll be pleased to have your company, Matthew. Orinda and I will be happy knowing that the children will have a teacher when we get there. We were just talking about how Poultney is growing, so you'll probably get a good price for your spread."

Any excitement that I may have felt about the coming trip seemed to melt away. *Oh, no,* I thought, *those boots, the right one with the patch on its toe and the left with the worn-down heel, will be following me to Ohio!*

With all of the preparations for the move, the height of summer had passed before we knew it, and the August heat, like a hot oven, roasted us for weeks on end. Ma speculated, "I'm not going to try to can the perishable vegetables for the trip west. Why don't we just eat the vegetables that would spoil and dry the beans and peas? We can put the apples in large barrels. And the children can dig the potatoes, put them in sacks and store them on wooden planks in the cool root cellar to keep them from rotting. I think we can take carrots, turnips and cabbages. I'll use them up first along the way."

Pa nodded. "And I have some men coming in two weeks for the threshing."

The next morning Ma started retching and having stomach cramps.

Pa looked worried. "Abby, come help Ma. I think we need the midwife. I'm going to get my horse, and quick as a wink I'll fetch Granny Colder."

When she wasn't boiling water and laying out clean cloths, Abby sat with Ma in her bedroom. We all walked around quietly and whispered. Pa came back around noon, and Granny Colder followed him in her buggy. Granny was a small woman with white hair and a neat, clean apron still fastened around her waist. She must have come directly from her kitchen. Carrying a little black bag, Granny went directly to Ma's room and closed the door.

Pa urged, "You young'uns go out and weed the vegetable patch. Bring Abby some fresh vegetables to fix for dinner."

We knew he just wanted us out of the way, so we went. After some minutes we kept going back to the house one after another on some flimsy excuse to see how Ma was doing. I had just tiptoed into the house when Granny Colder came out of Ma's bedroom. She went over to Pa who was seated by the fire. "Mr. Howe, I think you should go into town and get Dr. Smith.

Pa blanched. "But Granny Colder, you've always delivered our babies. What's happened now?"

"The baby seems to be turned," she replied, "and I don't want to take a chance of giving your wife childbed fever by going in and turning the baby on my own." Granny patted him on the arm. "Now, don't you fret. Orinda is strong, and she'll be all right. I'd just feel better if Dr. Smith had a look at her."

"But, we've never had any trouble, Granny. Must I leave my wife?

Granny Colder drew up her five-foot height and commanded, "Mr. Peter Howe, I don't have time to argue, and don't you question me. You just get on that horse and go bring Dr. Smith. Now, git!"

I'd never heard anyone speak to Pa like that nor seen him move so quickly. He got on his horse and took out as if the devil himself were after him.

Eliza had been out feeding the chickens and knew the baby must be coming when she saw Pa ride toward the house with Granny Colder. She told us later that on seeing Pa heading back into town at breakneck speed she knew something must be wrong and called out to Squire Prouty, "I just saw my father riding pell mell toward town. I'd best run over to the farm to find out what's happening with Ma and see if I can be of help to Granny Colder."

When Abby saw Eliza standing at the door, she rushed over and hugged her. "Thank heavens you've come. Granny declares the baby is turned, and Pa's gone to town for Dr. Smith."

Eliza hugged her back, looked over her shoulder and saw me standing by the door, speechless. She came and put her arm around my shoulders. "It's going to be all right, Lucy. Granny is just very conservative and doesn't want to take any chances. She must have scared Pa though. Granny's really impressive when she gets her back up isn't she? Don't worry, Honey, Ma's going to be all right."

I went out back of the house, sat on a rock and started to cry. So much was happening so fast. I was feeling alone and scared when

Cyrus dropped down beside me. He didn't mutter anything, just sat there. After a while he gave my shoulder an awkward pat that made me feel better. We didn't move until we heard Pa's horse and the doctor's buggy coming up the lane.

Dr. Smith went inside, and we could hear him giving orders. "Bring soap and hot water. Wash your hands really well. Help me turn her on her side!" Granny Colder flew around doing as the doctor bid. Abby brought water and soap. Pa paced the floor. Cyrus and I felt scared as we listened to the constant undercurrent of moaning from Ma. When Eliza saw us through the door, she sensed some activity might distract us and suggested, "I think you had better go and help the others in the vegetable garden. I'll call you when the baby comes."

We scooted off and worked for the best part of an hour before Sarah stopped and held up her hand. "I think I heard a baby cry!"

We all dropped our hoes and ran for the house. Abby sat in the rocker holding a little baby wrapped in a clean blanket. We could see Pa in the bedroom sitting beside Ma, who was sleeping. Dr. Smith had just washed all the way up to his elbows and had a large towel in his left hand. He smiled when he saw us. "We had a very stubborn little girl who didn't want to be born just yet," he confided. "She's fine now, but your mother is weak. She'll need to rest, but she'll be just fine, too, in a week or so.

We gave a huge sigh of pure relief, and I felt like crying again. Eliz suggested "You'd best keep out of Ma's room so she can sleep. She's plain tuckered out. Come and take a peek at the new wee one." She was so very little. I had a hard time believing any of us had been so small. Her hands looked like tiny claws, and she was making mewing sounds with her lips just like Lady's pups did.

After a while, Pa joined us. "She's wrinkled like a little old lady isn't she? But soon she'll be fat and running around like you all. We're going to call her Claire."

Eliza stayed on for a few days to help out. One morning, about five days after Claire was born, she announced, "I think Ezra needs me at home. He's getting tired of fixing his own food." I hated to see her go. She was always so sparkly and fun.

Pa was right about the baby growing quickly. In no time, she was sleeping through the night. She had lots of family to look after her. The best time was when Ma was well enough to eat with us. We felt as if we were having a party and things were back to normal.

In another week, the grain was ready for harvesting and the corn for cutting. Pa confided, "I've arranged for some of the men in the neighborhood to come and help us out tomorrow." Pa had lent a hand to some of those men with jobs like breeding sheep, the fall harvest and barn raising. Now it was his turn to get some help.

Early the next morning, six strong men turned up at our house with sharp knives and their cradle-scythes, whose long blades were attached to several wooden slats. As the blades cut the wheat, the wooden slats caught it and held it until a pile had accumulated. "We're lucky with this sunny weather," Pa commented. "We'll start on the back forty." Among the six were the three men who would be going to Ohio with us plus three others I had seen at meeting. One fellow, a big Swede named Lars who lived just outside of town volunteered, "I'll set in." So he started swinging his cradle-scythe, and the others followed. They circled nearly eight acres cutting the stalks in the morning. They stopped now and again for some cider that Abby and Becky had carried out and placed in the corner of the field. Lars eyed Becky, whose golden curls reflected the sunlight. He seemed to drink most of the cider. She ignored him.

Each man went forward in his turn until the wheat field was cut. They bound the loose piles of wheat with twine. Ordinarily the men would have made shocks by setting every five or six bundles upright and spreading the stalks of two more bundles over them, to protect the grain from wet weather. We always left the shocks in the fields until late fall or winter when we were ready to thresh out the grain. But because we would be gone before winter set in, Pa needed to do the threshing earlier, so we children followed behind and loaded the bundles on a wagon ready to take them back to the barn.

"I get to ride in the wagon," I shouted as we all tumbled in.

"Pa, can I drive the team?" Cyrus asked.

"Maybe next year," Pa looked at Cyrus appraisingly.

"We won't be here next year!

"Well, I'm sure we'll be growing grain in Ohio," Pa answered as he flicked the reins to urge the horses forward.

In the barn, we spread the stalks out on the floor and picked up flails made of two hickory sticks joined together by hide. Holding the longer stick and swinging down sharply on the stalks, we separated the heads of grain from the stalks.

Putting the wheat heads on a long wooden winnowing tray, we held on to the handles and tossed the grain up in the air to let the wind blow the chaff away. We never wasted anything and would use the stalks or straw for bedding for the animals or to fill our bed tickings. Sarah and I had fun tossing the screen. "Let's see how high we can make it go!" I cried.

Pa stuck his head through the barn door. "Lucy! You're spilling grain all over. This is not a game, young lady! I have a lot on my mind now, and I want you to settle down!" I was hurt. Why didn't he speak to Sarah? Well, in all honesty, I had to admit, it was my idea to toss the screen higher. I guess Pa knew Sarah wouldn't do that on her own.

After several days, all of the wheat and barley had been cut. Pa announced, "You've each done a good job. Tomorrow we'll go to the corn field." Luckily, the good weather held. The men cut the ears from the stalks with long knives. We children gathered the ears in baskets and carried them to the barn. There we husked by hand the corn that we were going to grind or feed to some of the animals. My fingers and the palms of my hands were sore and red.

The work lasted two weeks, and during that time Abby, Eliza and Becky prepared large noonday meals for the men in the fields. They started early in the morning peeling apples, scrubbing vegetables and carrying wood for the stove. Eliza fried chicken. Abby rolled out dough made from flour, lard and water. Becky fried sausages and bacon. Wonderful smells began to rise about ten o'clock. The men came in at noon to a table laden with platters of crispy chicken, sizzling ham and sausages, heaping bowls of green beans, carrots and peas swimming in butter. Apple, fruit and berry pies and dumplings were in the middle of the table for dessert. I always was amazed how the table, full when the workers came in, would be bare when they left.

Ma helped when she could, and each day she got stronger. Cyrus, Thomas and I washed dishes and carried out sandwiches and cider to the men in the field in the afternoons. I liked washing dishes best when I could blow the soap bubbled out at Cyrus and Thomas. I always felt those days were like a celebration, like Christmas in July and August, with the large meals and lots of people milling about. Everyone seemed so happy and busy.

One of the men, a large fellow with dark hair and eyes and a bad complexion took a shine to Becky. We all laughed at her trying to stay out of his sight. I whispered to Sarah, "I'm going to tell him to stop Becky when she comes out to the field and tell her, 'I am a rich Southerner in disguise. I have a thousand acres in Virginia and am looking for a wife.'"

I didn't know Eliza was standing behind me and heard me. "I don't think you'd better do that, Young Lady. You could get into a peck of trouble starting with me!" So I didn't. I would do anything for Eliza.

The day after the harvest was all in, Pa hitched the team to the wagon and beckoned to us to pile in around the many sacks filled with corn and wheat. We were taking the grain sacks to Uncle Silas's gristmill to be ground into flour or corn meal. The corn or grain Pa didn't have ground would be used for food for the animals or to trade for provisions to take with us to Ohio.

The mill, located on a stream north of town, was a big wooden building. The water from the stream had been redirected so that it ran into a long, narrow millrace, where it picked up speed and turned a huge wooden waterwheel as it flowed rapidly back into the stream. The noise of the roaring water and the creaking wheel were so loud we couldn't hear each other talk. The big outside wheel was attached to other wheels inside the mill that turned two large round stones.

The whole building shook and trembled when the large millstones turned round and round, grinding the corn into meal and the grain into flour.

Everything in the mill was covered in a fine dust. We all squatted down and wrote our names in the dust on the floor. I kept writing the word "Ohio," which Pa explained means great river. Silas Howe was all covered in the white flour dust too—his clothes, his eyebrows, and his beard. Only his eyes stood out as dark brown spots. Pa stood and talked to Uncle Silas while the flour and meal were poured back into the sacks. Pa took a long time shaking Uncle Silas's as if he'd never see him again. Maybe he wouldn't. After we bid farewell to Uncle Silas, we loaded the heavy sacks into the wagon and headed for home.

As the moon rose each evening, I felt a certain sadness. Pa came out on the front porch one night and sat beside me. The cool night air ruffled my hair. The last of the night crickets made a clicking noise. They'd be gone with the first frost. The lightning bugs were already long gone. I put my head on Pa's shoulder. He asked in a gentle voice, "What's the matter, Lucy?"

I was trying not to cry. "I think I'll miss the Vermont moon, Pa."

He laughed. "Lucy, the moon shines in Ohio just like it does here. I bet it's even prettier there."

"I don't think it could be, Pa. I don't think it could be."

CHAPTER SEVEN

SAYING GOOD-BYE FOREVER

66 "I always thought this family was overworked, but these last few weeks have been just crazy!" Becky wailed. "What is all this frenzy about killing ourselves to get ready to go to Ohio? Why couldn't we just wait until next year?" She stormed around the two large pieces of linen and tow-cloth that she and the girls had woven in strips and sewn together. "We're going to have to carry these heavy pieces of cloth to town and get them painted to make the material waterproof. I hope we can use a wagon Can you imagine how hard it will be to cover the wagons with the cloth."

"But it will protect our food, household goods and even ourselves from the wind, the rain and the sun while on the long trek to Ohio. Pa's purchased two two-horse wagons and Squire Prouty got one for himself and Eliza so we'll need lots of cover! Stop complaining," Ma scolded.

Ma wasn't paying much attention to Becky. She went on talking to herself, making a list. "I'm putting the clothes we're going to take in a large canvas bag. Most of the wagon will be filled with necessities . . . blankets, pillows, and ticking. We'll take some iron kettles so we can cook outdoors. Pa can attach the kettles to the outside of the wagon on hooks. He can put the washtubs and lanterns on hooks too. We'll take the horses of course. But not the other animals." She looked at Cyrus. "Yes, you can take Lady. A watch dog will come in handy. But you'll have to give away her pups. We just won't have enough food."

"But, Ma, Lady can catch chipmunks and mice and feed the pups."

Ma snapped, "No." That was the end of that discussion.

Ma was a little put out herself. Pa had informed no furniture! "No, Orinda, we don't have room. I can make new furniture when we get there. I just need to take my tools." Yes, I thought, the saws, axes, shovels, spades, hammers and all the rest would take up a good deal of space. He'll have to take his rifle and gunpowder too.

"Maybe just my rocking chair," she countered. "You made that when Abby was born, and I've rocked all the children in it."

"Well, all right, but just that chair! Cyrus, come and help me bring in some wood!" Whenever Pa got frustrated, he brought in more firewood.

Ma looked sadly at the wooden chairs. Some had seats made of braided cornhusks. She and Pa had spent a good deal of time braiding dried husks together with overlapping husks to make a long string. She had woven the seats zigzag back and forth onto chair frames that Pa had made. Two of the chairs had seats that Pa fashioned of split ash. He had woven our baskets from the split ash too. "Well, I can take some of the baskets," she consoled herself. "They can hang on the outside of the wagon too.

"The neighbors are coming over next Monday to wish us well," she continued. "They offered they'd each bring something, but I would like to have some simple fare to offer them in return." Ma wrinkled her forehead.

"Why not make a big pot of soup? We can use up all the fresh vegetables that we won't be taking with us," Abby suggested looking up from where she was folding the large wagon covers.

Ma brightened. "That's a good idea, and we could make apple tarts. The apples have come ripe, and we surely can't take all of them. Becky, could you sort out the apples that we haven't packed in the barrels and start making up the pies?"

"Do you have any more bright ideas for work that I could do before I fall down dead, Abby?" Becky stomped out of the room.

Little Claire was lying on a pallet on the floor. She was six weeks old and could turn over on her back or stomach. Ma nursed her several times a day, and she was filling out nicely. She wasn't paying any attention to the hubbub going on all around her.

"Cyrus, have you made the bows to curve over the wagon beds?" Pa asked as they each dumped an armload of wood by the fireplace. "We'll need them strong enough to hold the heavy canvas covers." Seeing the blank look on Cyrus's face, Pa offered kindly, "Come on, son. Let's find some stout hickory. We'll do it together."

For the rest of that week before we were to leave, we all worked night and day to get ready.

Ma kept finding more things to do. "What if it rains and we can't build a fire?" she mused. "What will we do for light? I think we'd be right smart to make some more candles. The weather will be cool, so we won't have to worry about them melting in the wagon."

So Sarah and I were put to work at that chore. There was a lot of fat—scraped from inside the skins and around the guts—left from butchering, so we put it in a big kettle and brought it to a boil. While the fat simmered for several hours, we knitted strings for the candlewicks.

To give Sarah a break, I sighed, "Why don't you so outside for a little while and find some straight tree branches. I'll stay here and keep an eye on the fire so it doesn't get too hot." The smell of rancid fat hung heavy in the air. When Sarah returned, we tied six strings—about eight inches long and about two inches apart—to each branch before straining the hot fat through a sack to get liquid tallow. We dipped the strings into the kettle until each was thinly covered with the waxy residue. When we lifted the branches away from the pot, we straightened the coated strings and hung the branches over benches allowing the tallow to harden. We had to move right smart when we dipped again so the tallow already on the strings didn't melt. We kept going until Ma decided, "The candles are fat enough, girls. Cut the strings off the branches and put the candles in a bag as soon as they're cool."

When the day of the send-off party came, neighbors from all around came to bid good-bye. We were all so tired from getting ready to depart; I thought we'd go to sleep talking to people. But because we'd be leaving early the next day and they would have their morning chores to do, it was the last chance we'd have to bid each other farewell.

Our table groaned with the food everyone had brought. A big kettle filled to the brim with soup hung on the crane in the fireplace. Our friends had brought their own cups and plates, and each person filled them with soup and vittles. Pa had set a large keg of cider at the corner of the table so folks could wash out their cups and fill them with cider after they'd finished their soup.

As for Mrs. Rath—none other than the Widder Croaker—she was holding forth in a corner of the living room. She had taken the only chair by the fireplace. Everyone else was standing about or sitting on stools, benches or the floor. The children were running around outside while it was still light. With the coming of autumn, the days were getting shorter.

"Well, Clara Putnam, are you ready to face those Indians? I hear they've perpetrated some savage massacres," Widder Croaker offered and sat back with a satisfied air. Wasn't that just like her—full of big words, conjuring disaster and causing distress?

Poor Clara Putnam's weak blue eyes grew large. She spoke in a thready voice to her husband. "George, have you heard about massacres?" She looked frantically around for her two children. Were they safe? She saw them playing hopscotch in the mud with Cyrus and me.

"Miz Rath, there was a massacre in 1781. Law, that was twenty years ago," Mr. Putnam groaned. "You gotta remember that Lt. Col. David Williamson brought that on hisself. The Indians were getting even since he went in and killed a lot of Moravian Christian Indians of the Delaware tribe. Those were peaceful men, women and children, who were just out working in the fields. It's not only the Indians that have got some mean men."

"How many tribes are there in the Ohio Territory, Putnam?" A stout farmer from the other side of town inquired.

"I don't rightly know all of them, Bill. There's the Iroquois and Wyandots or Hurons in the North and the Miami People in the west," George Putnam explained to Mr. Davis, counting them off on his fingers. "In the east, where we'll be going, there are the Delaware and the Shawnee. The Delaware tribe rightly ought to be called the Lenapes."

"Isn't that Chief Tecumseh a Shawnee?" Mr. Davis asked. "I hear he's out trying to stir up the tribes. He's up and down the territory, working for the Brits."

Pa heard the talk and saw the sheer terror on Clara Putnam's face. He walked over and put his hand on Mr. Putnam's shoulder. "Well, George, the army has got lots of forts set up. The soldiers can protect us as long as we mind the treaties and don't try to squat on Indian Territory." Taking Pa's hint that he should drop the conversation that had his wife in a state, he stood up and went to the table to refill his plate and cup.

"Where you planning on settling, Peter?" It was Bill Davis again. The hefty farmer was a real question box. Pa never cared for being grilled.

"Eastern Ohio Territory, near Marietta," he barked.

"I heard land donated from New York, Virginia and Connecticut has been cut up into seventeen different parcels," Mr. Davis stated. "Some of that land belongs to land grant companies, some's to be given as fire rewards to people the Brits burned out in the Revolution or to military veterans as pay for military service, some's owned by Congress. A real mess! Who will you buy your land from? How much does it cost?"

"The Public Land Act did a good job surveying the land and laying it out in sections," Pa replied. "I'll get my acreage from the

Ohio Land Company. They have an office in Fort Campus Martius at Marietta. The family'll stay near there while I get the land and build a house. The land's a real bargain, at a few dollars an acre. We'll get in early on. If you decide to come out later, Davis, you'll have to pay a good deal more." Pa seemed to like that thought. He smiled. Mr. Davis looked flustered.

"The letters we've been getting back from the folk there are glowing about how fertile the land is. No rocks to dig out. Fruit trees, all kinds, apples and peaches. The winters are mild compared to Vermont's. I'll think of you in a blizzard in January when I'm enjoying a light rain or snow. Have you got all your crops harvested, Bill?" Pa paused.

"Yep. Finished last week. You must have had to scurry to get yours all in and get packed up. Did you get a good price on your land? How much?"

Minerva must have seen Pa getting red in the face. She quickly stepped up beside him and said, "I think we need more cider, Pa. Have you tried the apple tarts, Mr. Davis? There aren't many left." From his size, Mr. Davis didn't need any more food. However, the thought that he might miss out on some sent him scurrying to the table.

Widder Croaker loved to exaggerate, which made her a good storyteller as well as a gossip. She had gathered a group of small children around her and was in the middle of a tale. "The night was so black no moon or stars shone, and the wind had picked up," she intoned with all the drama she could muster. 'The settlers—my mother's family—were huddled in their little cabin in the forest. No other farmers for miles around. The family needed more wood for the fire and water to drink, but was afraid to go out. They heard the howls of the wild Indians and the wolves. Chills went up their spines. My own mother was just a child and was scared out of her wits!"

The children were sitting in a circle, all scared to death, their mouths hanging open.

Harris Rath stood outside the circle of children. "But, Grandma," he interjected, "didn't you tell me that your ma grew up in a big house in Philadelphia?"

It was no secret that Widder Croaker loved her grandson above all the rest of her family, but at times he was trying. Sweet but unimaginative and a bit dim, he persisted, "Well, didn't she, Grandma? You described the fancy clothes she had and how they had nice china dishes. Isn't that so? Weren't you telling the Hobbses how rich she was? How she gave that all up to marry great grandpa Rath and live here in Vermont with him and his family."

The children looked from Widder to Harris, doubt in their eyes. "Well, if she had lived in a cabin in the woods, that is the way it would have been," the Widder mumbled. The spell was broken. But just as the children started to move away, Minerva called, "They're playing hide and seek out front. If you want to find who's "it" before dark, you'd best go!" The children left in a hurry.

"I really admire your adherence to the truth, Harris." She was laughing.

Harris blushed. "I'm going to miss you a lot, Minerva. Nobody else says nice things about me."

"I could write you a letter, if you like. I can tell you all about Ohio and if there are wild Indians. What grows there. What the weather is like." Minerva sat down beside him.

Harris hesitated, "I'm not so good about writing back, spelling and all."

"This would give you a good chance to practice. You can tell me all about what's happening here. What all the folk are doing, all the news."

"I'd really like that Minerva." He hesitated, and gulped, "I made you a going-away present." He reached in his pocket and took out a little wooden bracelet. He had smoothed the curves on the circlet with such care that not a rough place could be found. On the front of the wooden band was a little blue bird—wings spread and head tilted—whittled out of the lightest wood "You once told me that bluebirds was your favorite of all animals and birds."

"Oh, Harris, it's just lovely and the first jewelry I've ever had. Thank you so much. I'll think of you every time I wear it. Look, Ma, what Harris made for me." Ma sat down on the bench beside Minerva.

Harris flamed red with embarrassment. Ma looked at the bracelet in Minerva's hand. "Why, Harris, you have a real talent. What a kind and thoughtful gift for a friend," she replied, with emphasis on the word friend.

Widder Croaker had been taking in all of the preparations for our departure. She turned to Ma. "Are you going to go through with this foolishness, Orinda? You with a six-week-old baby and having such a hard time with the delivery? Your man speculated he might take the wagons overland to the Allegheny and go down the river. You can't stand that journey! You'll never live to see Ohio. And even if you do, that little baby won't make it. Such a journey will kill it!"

Ma's face had gone white, and her lips formed a thin line. In a cold voice, she retaliated, "Thank you for your concern, Harriet. I think I'll make it just fine." She smiled, "Really, I won't have to clean the house or make beds. We'll just have two wagons to take care of. We'll eat simple meals and our men will get the firewood and drive the wagons. I'll just ride and keep an eye out for the children. It will be a real treat."

"Well, I never!" the Widder sputtered. "I hope you know what you're doing. Come on Harris. We'd best be getting home. You have the milking to do." But the thought of going home to chores, milking, baking, cooking and all had got to the Widder. I could tell Mrs. Rath was thinking over what Ma had uttered. She went to the table and rescued her raisin pie on the blue and white china plate she was always bragging about as part of her Grandma's china.

That night, when everyone had left and we children were all in bed in the loft, I could hear Pa snoring from the bedroom downstairs. I peeked over the rim of opening and saw Ma walking around the house, touching the furniture, looking out the windows. She fingered the white curtains. Her face and tightly braided hair were reflected in the window pane. She ran her hand along the table and straightened the cracked blue and white water pitcher. The fire crackled in the last embers of the back log in the fireplace and threw her shadow over the wall as she bent her head. I think she whispered good-bye to her house and her home forever.

CHAPTER EIGHT

OVERLAND TO
THE RIVER

O n the ninth of September, we got up while it was still dark and
finished the last-minute preparations. Pa and the girls fastened
the painted tow-cloths on the wooden ribs that arched over the
wagons. Pa called, "Abby, pull the back of each of those coverings
tight and draw them into a circle by a cord threaded through a hem
at that end of the tow-cloth. On chilly or rainy days, we'll draw the
cords tight to keep out the water and cold. But on warm days, we'll
make the openings bigger to let air flow through."

Becky and Sarah gathered the straw tickings and put them in the
wagon beds along with sheets, quilts and pillows. Pa fastened his
toolbox securely to the left side panel of the second wagon. Cyrus
and Thomas hung the tin tubs, iron kettles and lanterns on hooks at
the sides of the wagons and tied them so they wouldn't fall off if the
roads were rough. The clanging and rattling would have wakened
the dead. Pa bound Ma's precious rocking chair to the tailgate of
one wagon. Ma carefully laid the family Bible under the seat in the
front wagon.

Sarah and I hung salted hams from the ribs of the wagons, and Pa and Abby crammed barrels of apples, potatoes, turnips, carrots, cabbages and cornmeal into every spare space. Pa hung his gun and powder horn from a rib in the wagon he would drive. A large box under the wagon had the feed corn for the horses. They would get about a half-pound a day. Pa was counting on them to eat grass wherever we stopped.

We made breakfast out of the leftovers from the neighbors' send-off, and ate in silence, sitting on the stools and benches we'd never see again. "I'll pack up what's left for a picnic lunch," Ma called.

The sun was just rising when we pulled out of the barnyard and began our long southwesterly trek for Ohio. Pa was driving one wagon with Becky beside him. Ma was driving the other wagon with Abby seated next to her. Baby Claire was asleep on a straw ticking directly behind Ma, but the rest of us children crawled to the rear of our wagons to gaze through the circles of canvas. As our house receded from sight, I turned around to see how Ma was holding up. She sat on the front seat with the reins in her hands, the Bible at her feet. Her back was straight, her eyes on the road ahead. Little wisps of gray hair fluttered out from under her bonnet. She never looked back.

As we turned out of our lane, we met Eliza and Squire Prouty whose wagon, like ours, was loaded with as many of their belongings as they could carry. Mr. Stacey followed along in a smaller wagon.

Pa had cleared a good deal of our land. The trees that remained along the road were just beginning to put on their fall colors. We noticed the swamp maples because they change color first in the fall to a burning crimson. The yellowing leaves of the black and green ash already were beginning to drop. After we left, the sugar maples would be a striking combination of yellow and red, but not the bright reds of the swamp maple. I wouldn't be there to see the oaks turn rusty orange or red, and brown. I thought, I won't see the snow either. Will there be snow in Ohio? How deep? Will it be all forest?

I was startled out of my reverie when Sarah poked me in the side and sniffed, "Move your foot. It's sticking me in the back." Things got lively as the Putnams, the Hopsons and the Prindles pulled out onto the road with their wagons, children and an assortment of dogs and joined our little caravan.

We stopped by a stream at lunchtime for a picnic. Ma passed out cold leftovers. The sun was hot, so when Pa took the horses to the stream for a drink, we tagged along and waded in the creek. "If you want, you young'uns can walk alongside the wagons, as long as you don't stray off," Ma warned when we pulled our stockings and shoes on again. She wiped off the last of the tin plates and climbed back into the wagon. She looked tired.

After Pa had rehitched the team, we ran or walked beside the wagons. Late in the afternoon we saw a chestnut tree growing by the side of the road. We'd never seen chestnuts growing, so we stopped and filled a basket with them. Mr. Stacey explained, "You're supposed to roast them. I promise to show you how tonight." The day passed slowly, and I was glad when, just before dark, we stopped for the night. The men quickly erected a shelter. They drove some wood crotches into the ground, lashed a pole across them and laid branches slanting along one side of the pole. They spread one of the painted wagon covers over the makeshift frame.

We children pulled up all the grass in a big circle. Pa and Squire Prouty set a big log from the forest in the middle of the circle. They laid wood—first twigs and next larger limbs—against this log and started a fire. A couple of men went into the woods and shot some grouse. When they had removed all the feathers and insides, they put the birds on a metal rod and propped the rod over the fire. Every so often they turned the rod. The fat dripped into the fire with a spitting noise.

Ma and all the women got out their spider skillets and cooked the rest of the dinner. My, but I had a good time smelling the wood smoke and the roasting grouse. Abby made corncakes. She mixed some water and cornmeal until it was stiff. She rolled the batter into balls and flattened them out between her palms. Ma put some lard into one of skillet, and Abby fried the corncakes over the fire. When everything was ready, we ate together—all thirty of us.

Some of the folks sang songs or hymns as we watched the fire die down. When the embers were a red glow but no flames could be seen, Mr. Stacey continued, "All right, the fire looks good to roast the chestnuts. Where are they?"

We brought out the basket of nuts, and Stacey pulled a sharp knife out of his pocket. "First, you have to make a slit of about a half inch in the shell opposite the flat side. That lets the steam out so they don't explode when you cook 'em." He took a beat-up old skillet with holes in it out of his pack adding, "I use this to pop corn, too." He smiled. I'd never seen Mr. Stacey so relaxed. In fact, I don't remember ever seeing him smile in school.

"The reason you need holes in the pan is that the chestnuts release steam as they cook." Every once in a while he took off the lid and rolled the chestnuts around. After about fifteen minutes the shells turned black and he deemed them done. "Here, see what you think of roasted chestnuts." Stacey emptied the nuts on a tin plate and handed them to Abby. She blushed, took one and handed the pan to Ma who passed them all around. We peeled off the shells and ate the tender, toasty nutmeats. What a treat! Ohio had great possibilities and we weren't even there yet!

"Since it's pleasant tonight, we can sleep outside," Pa observed. "You children gather lots of leaves." When we each had made a big pile, Pa pulled the straw tickings out of the wagon and put them on top of the leaves. Ma covered us with the quilts. I went to sleep looking up at the stars. I dreamt I was a princess sleeping on a bed of feathers.

We soon rolled from Vermont into the wilderness of New York State. Each day after that followed the same pattern as the first few for the next three hundred miles. One day we saw four hunters come out of the woods carrying a pole with three deer strung up by their hoofs. Pa stopped to talk to them.

"Look's like the shooting is good around here," Pa called from the lead wagon.

"Not a bad day's hunting. We got three deer. Could have had four more, but we only needed three. Should do well by our families for a while. Where're you bound for?" the tallest man with a brown beard asked.

"We're heading for the Ohio Territory," Pa replied.

"You might want to cut through the woods. Right here is a good place, if you want to go any ways by water. It's only about thirty miles to the headwaters of the Allegheny. Get you some canoes and go down the river through Pennsylvania and on to Ohio. It's a lot cheaper and easier than going by land. You'll have to leave this road and follow mostly a bridle path."

One of the men, Joseph by name, spoke up, "Adam and I took all the deer we need. If you want, Josh here could take our deer home to our families, and we could go with you'ns through to the settlement. It's called King's Town. That's where you'd git canoes. Adam's sister lives there and is sickly. He was wantin' to go see her anyways."

"Much obliged for the advice and the offer. Let me talk to the others." Pa pulled up his wagon. He got down and went to parley with the rest of the folk. "What do you think? Should we go over to the river?"

"Any money we save on the traveling, we can use to buy more land," Mr. Hopson volunteered.

"If it's quicker, I second the yes." Mr. Putnam put in. "As long as it's safe," he added, looking at his wife.

"All right. We'll go by the river." Pa walked back to the hunters. "We'll take you up on your kind offer. Looks like we'll have to do some clearing of the woods to get the wagons through."

We went about ten miles that day. "Best make camp now," Mr. Putnam proposed. "The horses are tired, and Clara's getting wagon sore going over these bumpy trails." We all agreed to stop for the night.

One of the hunters, Adam, approached Pa after supper. "If it's all right with you," he asked, "I'm just going to walk on through to the settlement. I can make it in a day, but the wagons will take two days. Joseph will be with you and is an able guide."

Ma spoke up, "If some of the girls will go with me, I think I'd like to walk to the settlement too and get some exercise."

Minerva and Becky volunteered to go with Ma. So they started off with Adam the next morning, Ma carrying the baby. Pa turned to me, "Lucy, would you like to ride up here on the front seat with me?"

"Oh, yes Siree!" I happily took my seat. In the other wagon, Sarah sat up front with Abby, who had taken over the driving from Ma. As we jogged along, I asked Pa, "At that party, you talked about the Public Land Act. Does that law tell people how to govern the Ohio Territory?"

"Why, Lucy, I didn't know you knew anything about governing a place. Where did you learn about that?" We were going at a snail's pace, so Pa let the reins hang loose while we talked.

"I heard some men at the party talking." I felt quite proud of myself.

"Well, Honey, the Public Land Act just states how the territory will be laid out, so when a family buys land they'll know what the boundaries are. The law that sets up the governing is the Northwest Ordinance. Now that's a very important piece of work. It was passed in 1787 and proclaims that all that land would be governed by Congress and owned by public domain. That means owned by the people of the United States."

"Is there a president of the territory, Pa? Why didn't they call it a colony?"

"Nope, a governor would govern the territory. The English called their land parcels colonies. The Americans didn't want any references that smacked of England, so they called the place a territory. The Ordinance provides for a secretary and judges, and decrees once there are five thousand free males over the age of twenty-one, they can elect a legislature."

"Oh, my gosh, five thousand is a lot of people." I was impressed.

"Yep, it sure is, but there are that many there now. When they get sixty thousand people, they can start the business of becoming a state. An interesting point here, if they do become a state, they'll have equal rights with the original states."

I laughed, "I bet that makes the original colonies mad. I know it would me. Like saying baby Claire has the same place as me."

"You bet it does. But think of it this way, Claire has as much of a place in the family as you or Cyrus."

"But she can't do any chores or help out!" I could see the argument from the point-of-view of the old colonies.

"But pretty soon she will. She might have some qualities that the rest of us don't have, like patience." Pa looked at me out of the corner of his eye. "The Ordinance has a lot of other worthwhile provisions like: freedom of religion, trial by jury and freedom from slavery. It also states land can't be taken from the Indians without their consent. I sure hope they follow that one, or we could be in for a heap of trouble." Pa fell silent and so did I. The thought of being equal with Claire and Thomas made me angry. It came to me that by that same rule, *I was the equal of Eliza and Abby.* I held that happy thought through the rest of the day.

We spent two more nights on the trail. On the third day, we made it to the small community of only three or four families living near the river. It was called King's Town because a man named King had settled there first. There was no connection to the King of England.

We spent nine days in King's Town, where plans were laid for the rest of our trip. It was agreed that we should hire a man to help out. As the little town was on a creek only four miles from the Allegheny River, the men decided that they would make and launch canoes there. Pa said, "We can't take the horses in the canoes. We'll have to drive several wagons and take those horses the long way out to Marietta while the rest go on by river."

Squire Prouty volunteered, "Why don't Eliza, Mr. Hopson, the hired man and I take the horses and go the long way? We can meet you in Marietta."

Under her breath I heard Eliza whisper, "I think the children are getting to the Squire."

Pa offered, "Fine. We'll look for you when we get there." So the little party of four took the wagons and the extra horses and headed southwest the next day.

The men who remained in King's Town started to work making canoes. They chopped down six large trees and began digging out their insides. While they worked, we camped outside of the settlement. Every night, from the safety of our tents, I could hear the wolves howling. "Do you hear them, Cyrus?"

"Don't worry, Lucy," he responded. "Lady is a good watchdog. She'll tell us if any wolves come near."

"What will we do? She can't attack a whole wolf pack!"

"She's not supposed to attack. She just warns Pa. Pa will get his gun and shoot them. Now go to sleep!" I felt better that Lady was in our tent.

When they had finished the canoes, the men lashed every two of the dugouts together, making three pairs. We hefted the wagon wheels on top, letting them lie flat with their hubs wedged between the canoes to keep them steady. We all put our belongings into the canoes; got in and headed out.

"How many miles will we be on the river?" Mrs. Putnam asked her husband.

"I think it's about five hundred miles, Clara. But don't worry, we'll be fine."

"I think there are only two or three rapids," Mr. Prindle volunteered with a smile.

"John, don't," his wife whispered. "She's frightened enough."

"What's a rapid?" Clara Putnam asked.

"It's where the water moves swiftly over and around rocks or sometimes drops over a little ledge," Mr. Prindle answered quietly, somewhat ashamed of having purposely gotten Mrs. Putnam stirred up.

"George, have you ever seen rapids? Are the Indians friendly? What if we're on the river, will they chase us?" Clara Putnam began to ring her hands and cry.

"Now, now, Clara, don't get all worked up. These are friendly Indians. If we don't bother them, they'll just let us alone." He propped his oar on his leg and reached over to pat her hand.

Annoyed, Pa turned to us and changed the topic. "We'll pass some Indian settlements before long. You youngsters may get to see a papoose and the way the Indians live."

"Oh, my Lord! Indians and rapids! Oh, George, what have you gotten us into?" Mrs. Putnam wailed as we paddled out into the river.

CHAPTER NINE

A PASS WITH DEATH

W e enjoyed floating from New York down through Pennsylvania on the beautiful Allegheny with its big river bends and bluff banks. The current was swift in some places, so we moved fast. I liked to watch the fish darting about in the water. Sometimes I trailed my hand in the water. It was icy cold and so clear I even tried once to touch a fish. Every night we camped out on the shore of the river. Some of the men caught bass near the rocky bars or in the shallow flats. We had good fish suppers with cornbread, potatoes and carrots that we'd brought with us.

The fourth day out we came on the first of the rapids we were to encounter. Mr. Putnam was in the front of the canoe as a lookout for rocks, sunken logs and other troubles that lay ahead. Before long, he saw a boulder in the middle of the river and called out, "Steer to the right."

Just before we got to the jagged outcropping, he shouted, "No! No! We can't go to the right! Pull to the left!" With all our might we pulled the paddles to steer left, but the current was so powerful, it grabbed the canoes and turned them broadside against the huge rock. One dugout went up on the granite slab. The dugout that was attached to it broke loose and wedged into a rock outputting. Ma, Eva, Thomas and Sarah stayed in the canoe on the outcropping. Cyrus and I scrambled out onto its slippery surface. The people in the other canoes came alongside and got Ma's dugout back to the shallows. Cyrus and I had to wait on the boulder until they could unload another canoe, come get us and take us ashore.

We knew Ma and Pa would be spittin' mad that we hadn't stayed in the canoe. At that point, though, we were more scared of slipping off the rock then of being spanked. The rapid current made circles around us, and the wet surface was tricky under our feet. "Come here, Lucy. Hold my hand. I've got my foot wedged in a crevice of the rock. I think it will hold us until Pa can get one of the other canoes unloaded and come get us." Cyrus's voice was gruff. I held tight to his hand.

"Do you think there are any snakes in the river, Cyrus?" I remembered the day Sarah and I went berry picking.

"No. The current is too fast." I don't think he knew, but his answer made me feel better. The spray, when the water hit the rock, wet us all over. The wind blew on our wet clothes, and, because I felt chills and had started to shake, I had a hard time keeping hold of Cyrus's hand.

The people on the shore quickly unpacked a dugout. The noise of the water was so loud, though, that we couldn't hear anything they were yelling at us. Finally, we saw Pa and Mr. Stacey get in the canoe and start paddling toward us. When they'd pulled around to the side of the rock, Pa shouted, "Give me a hand, Lucy," I reached out and took his hand, and he lifted me into the canoe. "Now, Cyrus," he ordered, "edge over to this side and give me your hand."

Cyrus tried, but the rock was so slippery he started to slide. Pa's strong arm grabbed him just before he hit the water. We were both soaked and shivering. Mr. Stacey drew out the blanket that he'd brought with him and wrapped us up in it. Paddling against the current with powerful strokes, they brought us to shore. We were surprised neither Ma nor Pa uttered an angry word. "Sit here by the fire and get warm! I'll bring you some dry clothes," Ma suggested.

Mrs. Putnam was in tears. "Oh, George! They could have drowned! We all could have! I want to go home!"

"Now, now, Clara. They are fine. Why don't you get something for our children to eat? We'll be camping here for a day or two while things dry out."

Mr. Prindle and Mr. Putnam had rescued the canoe that broke loose. Nothing was lost as everything had been lashed tight, but everything was soaked. Pa and Mr. Prindle built a large fire while everyone unpacked the wet things and spread them out around the fire to dry. Mrs. Prindle helped Mrs. Putnam get some supper for her children. "You'd think it was her young'uns who'd had a close call, the way she carries on!" Ma snapped in a low voice to Pa.

"Now, Orinda, she has bad nerves," Pa answered in the same low tone.

"Humph!" Ma snorted.

Two days later we got all of our goods and supplies repacked and started downriver again. On the morning of the following day, we spotted an Indian camp near the shore. "Want to go up and see what their camp is like?" Pa asked.

"Not on your life. I'm sitting right here with our children," Mrs. Putnam declared. "You'd better stay here too, George, to protect us from those heathens."

"I'll remain with the canoes, Peter," Mr. Putnam added, "and guard the supplies, just in case the Indians get quizzical."

"You have nothing to fear from these Indians, Mrs. Putnam. They are Lenapes. The white men call them Delaware Indians," Mr. Stacey spoke quietly.

"Weren't they the Indians that tortured and killed Washington's friend Colonel Crawford?" Mr. Putnam asked, looking worried.

Mr. Stacy replied, "The story is that Moravian missionaries had converted some Delaware Indians to Christianity. The British moved those Indians from their village to Sandusky and took the Moravians away for a trial. Hungry, the Indians went back to their own village to harvest their crops. Some Pennsylvania militiamen under Lt. Col. David Williamson came on these people in their fields, and took them to the Indian's church where they spent the night. The next morning the Americans made the Indians kneel, crushed their skulls, scalped them and put all the bodies in a heap and burned them.

"Now, the Lenape are a peaceful people," Mr. Stacey continued, "even referred to as the grandfather tribe since they are the oldest of the Algonquian stock. But when they are hurt, they, too, can be cruel and ruthless. So they took their revenge on Col. William Crawford."

"But Colonel Crawford wasn't part of Williamson's action," Mrs. Putnam countered.

"No, but he was an American. We forget that our actions often are attributed to all the people we represent. Williamson killed twenty-eight men, twenty-nine women and thirty-nine children. How would you feel if that happened to your folk?" Stacey all but whispered.

We were all silent. Abby asked, "How do you know so much about the Lenape?"

"My parents were killed when I was a child . . ." Stacey started to answer.

Interrupting him, Mrs. Putnam gasped, "Did the Indians kill 'em?"

"No, it was the British." Stacey muttered.

Abby swallowed. "Oh, I am so terribly sorry." She reached out to touch Mr. Stacey's arm and quickly drew back.

"My parents had sent my brothers and sisters and me to hide in the woods. After a while we returned to our house, only to find that they were dead. And so we buried them. Although we children worked the farm and tried to get by on our own, we were always hungry. Some Lenape Indians had a settlement nearby. They shared food with us and helped us with the crops. When my sister was sick, one of the medicine men gave her some herbs that made her well. They are good people, and over time we got to know them well. But even with their help, we remained dreadfully poor."

I could think only of his patched boots and how I had made fun of them. I was ashamed of myself.

"Anyway, if you all want to see an Indian camp, I think we can go safely," Mr. Stacey suggested.

We trooped behind him up the hill to the camp. The houses in the camp were wooden frames covered with bark. They were square or oval in shape, and several families lived in each house. The little children were running around naked. The men wore breechcloths and moccasins. The women wore square wrap skirts from waist to knee and moccasins. All the clothes were made of soft deerskin. One man had a beautiful beaded bag hanging from his shoulder strap. I could see baskets and clay pots beside every house.

Stacey saw me admiring the clay pots. He explained, "Their pots have round bottoms. When used for cooking, they rest on three stones and a fire is built around them. I've seen pots big enough to hold and cook several deer."

Becky saw a papoose lying on a blanket. He was a sweet little baby with jet-black hair and eyes just asking to be cuddled. But when she picked him up, he started to cry. His mother came over, smiled at Becky and took the baby. He immediately stopped crying. Minerva grinned, "You don't seem to have the touch, Becky?"

Everything seemed orderly. Men were making bows and arrows. Several braves were digging out a canoe. I could see fields where corn and grain were growing. Mr. Stacey stopped and spoke to some of the men in a language that I couldn't understand. On the way back to camp, I asked him, "Do the Indians believe in God?"

"Yes. They believe in one God, but they also believe in lesser gods. They call them manëtuwak. I think the problem between the Indians and the white man is that the Indians think God owns the land and the air and the water and that people just use these gifts. The white man thinks he can own land. So when the white man gave the Indians trinkets, the Indians thought the white man wanted to use the land and the trinkets were tokens of thanks for letting them use the land. They had no idea they were selling land, because they didn't think they owned it."

"Come on, Lucy, we need to get back on the river," Pa called.

As I caught up with Pa at the canoe, I admitted: "Mr. Stacey isn't as bad as I thought."

Pa smiled. "I can see you're growing up, Lucy. I think he's a fine, strong, hard-working man, or I wouldn't let him be courting Abby."

Everything went well for several days. We floated downstream past great forests and through rolling hill country. Deep into autumn, all the trees had lost their leaves. The water was so clear I could see the rocky and sometime sandy bottom in the shallower stretches. As we rounded a bend in the river late one morning, the current suddenly quickened, and we heard a crunching noise! The two yoked lead canoes had run up on some large rocks lurking unseen below the surface of the churning water, and the side of one canoe had split off, as if a giant had snapped the sturdy vessel in two with his hands. The other canoe rose high in the air and toppled over! Men, women, children, goods, all spilled out into the shoulder-deep water! Each man and woman, struggling to keep their heads above water, made it to shore dragging two children, a child in each hand. Every one, that is, except Mrs. Putnam! She splashed to the bank wailing loudly, concerned only for herself.

Her oldest son, William, was still in the water. He got hold of a piece of the split canoe and pulled himself up on it just as his baby sister floated past him. Instinctively, he reached out. "I've got her, Pa!" he yelled. The other canoes rescued him and the baby. They proceeded downstream a ways, picking up whatever goods they could salvage.

On the bank, Mrs. Putnam was crying hysterically, "I told you, George, when we started, that I would never live to get to Ohio!"

Ma walked over, bent down and gave the wailing woman a good, sound slap in the face. Mrs. Putnam stopped crying and looked up, shocked.

"Oh, you'll live to get to Ohio, Clara. You're not dead yet!" As she walked away, I heard Ma mutter under her breath, "More's the pity!"

Pa looked over all of our companions and the remaining stores. "We were mighty lucky, Orinda. Nine children under eleven years old went into the river, and we saved them all! They're alive, safe and no one hurt. I think we've rescued most of our things too. They were in boxes and bundles and most of them floated. You boys dive down and get whatever you can find along the bottom. We've lost a canoe, though. Prindle, walk down the shore with me. Let's see if we can find a log to make ourselves a replacement."

As they started off, we spread the wet things on the grass. Mr. Putnam built a fire. Some of the goods we hung on tree limbs that we dragged over near the fire, but not close enough for the salvaged things to burn. We waited anxiously for Pa to come back. I remembered the Indian camp and hoped those Indians weren't mad at something some other Americans had done.

We all jumped when we heard a big "Hello!" from the river. Pa and Mr. Prindel were sitting in a canoe as big as two of ours together. A very tall, robust man with a red beard was with them. They beached the boat and came ashore shouting, "Good news! We ran into Mr. Sparks here about a mile down river. He has this here pirogue that he's willing to trade for our one good canoe, and we'll pay the balance."

Mr. Sparks gave us all a big smile that showed two missing front teeth. His clothes were covered with mud. "My family has gone back East, and I really don't need this big a canoe anymore. Just need one big enough to get my skins to market." He saw Becky and smiled again. She looked scared to death. "Where you headed?" Mr. Sparks asked, still looking at Becky.

Pa replied, "We're on our way to Marietta. Is it far?"

"Nope, with a little luck and no more accidents you should make it well within a week or two. I plan to come down to Marietta when the snow starts to fly and find a room. I just make do outside during the warm weather. I'll look in on you when I come." He glanced at Becky again.

"You're more than welcome." Pa shook hands. Mr. Sparks headed toward his newly acquired canoe, glancing over his shoulder again at Becky.

Minerva whispered in Becky's ear, "How lovely, Becky, that you're getting to meet some attractive and cultured people. I think he really likes you. If he comes to visit us in Marietta you'll have a friend!" Becky tossed her head and walked away but in the opposite direction of Mr. Sparks.

We had no more accidents the rest of our days on the river. We landed at our destination in Ohio on the twelfth of November, just about noon—nine weeks after we started our journey. Through the cold mists and light fog we could see the houses and Fort Campus Martius at Marietta. All of us were jumping up and down and hugging each other as soon as we beached. Clara Putnam started to cry.

"We made it," Ma sighed.

CHAPTER TEN

GROWING PAINS

P a gathered all our family around him. "I think we should have a moment of silent prayer to give thanks that we've made a safe trip." We bowed our heads. I could hear the birds singing and the voices of people in the houses or on the street. I glanced out the side of my eyes trying to spot some people. I'm sorry to admit that I was more curious than prayerful.

Pa cleared his throat and prayed. "Amen. This is a new beginning for us all. I think tonight before we go to bed, we should each review why we are here and where we want to go from now on. Find out what we want to accomplish with this new land. Now, enough talking! I'm going to go up to the fort to see about getting a house for us and inquire where we go to purchase land."

As he strode off, we pulled the canoes further up the shore and, wide-eyed, looked around at the town. It seemed big—lots more people than lived near us in Vermont.

Marietta is located where the Muskingum River flows into the Ohio and was the first town set up in the Northwest Territory. The river, like an ever-moving road, carried a lot of traffic—rafts, canoes like ours and boats of all kinds.

People walking by the waterfront on their way to town gazed at the river traffic, and several who stopped by to call hello asked where we were from. Ma commented to one woman who stopped to talk, "I've seen so many of those beautiful big trees like that one over there. They look something like the horse chestnut trees in Vermont."

"Lawsy, dear, those are our buckeye trees. We calls 'em that 'cause they look like the eye of a buck deer. Don't let your young'uns eat the nut. It's poisonous. Don't seem to bother the squirrels, though," she laughed. "My husband carries a buckeye in his pocket for good luck. You know yet where you're staying?"

"No, my husband went to ask about land and about a place to stay while we build a cabin." Ma smiled.

"Well, there's plenty of places, I tell you. Although there won't be for long! I've never seed a place grow so fast. Must be because of all the land that's available. Won't be long and we'll be a state. We came out from Massachusetts. Lots of folks come from New England. That's why this here town is laid out like those in New England, with four common areas and consideration for schools and churches. Folk are friendly here. Good luck to you!" She waved and went on her way.

Pa came back directly and spoke with great enthusiasm: "I've found an old blockhouse in a stockade up the Muskingum River about a mile from the Ohio. We can go there now and unload all our things. Tomorrow, we'll go up to the land office that's located right behind Fort Campus Martius and buy some land for ourselves. The other families have found accommodations too." Ma looked especially happy when he added, "I've also located a room for Squire and Eliza. He can start setting up a blacksmith's shop as soon as they get here and can get some land."

We waved our good-byes to the Putnams, the Hopsons and the Prindles. Ma seemed real relieved to be rid of Clara Putnam.

Back in our canoe, we headed up the Muskingum.

I didn't see many deer along the river since it was a short ride. I guessed with so many folks settling thereabouts, the deer were moving on like the Indians. Ma seemed pleased and relaxed. That is until she saw the blockhouse Pa had rented. We stood in dead silence looking around. The sides and floors of the small square house were made of yellow poplar slabs. Windows were cut out and covered with oiled paper.

"Where's the fireplace? Where do we cook?" Ma asked.

Pa seemed nervous as he explained, "These little houses don't have fireplaces. I'm told the women cook in the courtyard against the stumps of trees. But these are just places to rent, Orinda. The more ample houses are ones that people have built for themselves." Ma's lips had drawn into that thin line we all knew so well.

"Cook outside with winter coming on?" Ma quizzed.

Pa apologized, "It won't be all winter, Orinda. I'm going to town tomorrow and get some land. Quick as a wink, I'll get a house up and make you a proper fireplace. Prouty, Stacey and I have agreed to work together and help each other build our houses once we get some land."

Ma always had told us not to argue with what's done. But she turned away from Pa with a look on her face that put the fear of God in us. "All right, let's get those canoes unloaded. I don't see how we're all going to fit in here. Abby, Becky, Sarah and maybe Lucy can be boarded out and get some work. The young ones will stay here with me. I'll start asking around tomorrow about places for the girls. Hustle now. We want to unload before dark." We could tell Ma was in a bad mood, so we all scurried around. Pa built a fire outside and boiled some water. Abby added vegetables to make soup. The rest of us unpacked the canoes, lugged tickings in for beds and spread quilts. After supper that night, I lay awake thinking and asking myself why we had left the security of Poultney to come to this place.

"Are you asleep, Abby?" I whispered and rolled over until I could see her head outlined against the faint light coming in through the oilskin windows.

"No. What's the matter?" Her voice sounded somber and I thought she brushed away tears when she turned to talk to me.

Maybe she was feeling as forlorn as I was. I asked, "Where do you think I'll be boarded out to? I've never been away from home."

Abby reached out and took my hand. "Don't worry, Honey. Ma won't place you anywhere that isn't safe and good. You'll be close to us all the time and will get to come home every once in a while.

And we'll drop by to see you. It won't be long until Pa gets a house built, and we'll all be together again." I could tell by her voice that she was lying. She wanted to console me because I was younger but she was as worried as I was. What if Ma couldn't find us jobs? What if I had to go to an awful place? What if Pa couldn't get any land for a long time?

I went to sleep holding her hand.

After an early breakfast of leftover soup, Pa started for the land office to see about buying some acreage. Ma had set up the iron crane near a stump and was boiling a big kettle of water. "Girls, things got real dirty on the trip, so we're going to wash some clothes this morning. After breakfast we can hang them out to dry while we go to town to see about work. Becky, bring me some of the lye soap and we'll get started. Thomas, you and Cyrus gather firewood. You'll have to go outside the stockade and scout around to find some. I think other folk have gathered most within sight. Be right careful if you go into the woods. Lucy, you and Sarah can help them."

We spent most of the morning collecting logs and kindling and carrying load upon load back to the house. After lunch, I stayed with the younger boys, Eva and baby Claire, while Ma and the older girls went to town to find places to work. They came home all excited. Abby had found a job with a young farm couple who had a new baby and several small children. She was to look after the young'uns, cook and help the new mother with the housework. Becky had taken a place with the Treadwells, a prosperous older couple, as a seamstress. Minerva got a job as a cook for a large household and Sarah as a maid at the same place.

"Lucy, you will be doing chores for Major and Mrs. Coffer. You'll be washing dishes, sweeping the house, making beds, milking the cow—things like you do at home. You'll remember your manners," Ma commanded and went on. "She'll pay me thirty-three cents a week and give you board. You start the first of December. I think she wants someone to help out over Christmas. The military entertain a great deal over the holidays I hear."

My face fell. Eliza came over and put her arm around me. "It seems to be a nice place, Lucy. I met the lady with Ma. She seems likable. Minerva and Becky won't be far off. They'll be working for a military officer's family too." I felt a little better, but never had the days leading up to December been filled with so much anxiety.

Pa came home late in the evening. "Good news, Orinda. I've purchased a good many eight-acre lots laid out on the Muskingum River about four-and—a-half miles upstream. I'll get Stacey to help me start clearing tomorrow. We'll have a cabin up in no time. At supper, everyone seemed in a holiday mood, ready to celebrate the coming days. Everyone but me!

On December first, I packed my things in a shawl and started out, the dread in my heart increasing with every step of the four-mile walk. Mrs. Coffer met me at the tall front door of the house. "Wipe your shoes before you come in," was her brusque greeting. We're off to a bad start, I thought. I know enough to wipe my feet. "Come," she uttered, "I'll show you where you'll sleep. Bring your things." I followed her up the stairs to a small bedroom tucked under the eaves. "You'll share this room with Elsa. When you've unpacked"—she eyed my small bundle with pity—"come downstairs and set the table. We're having guests for dinner."

When she left the room, I sat down and cried. As Ma and Pa had trained me, when you have no choice, you face up to what has to be done. I wiped my eyes, untied the shawl and placed my few possessions on a shelf, and went downstairs. The house was nice, but not as big as some houses I saw while walking there—yet grand compared to our blockhouse. I peeked in the parlor as I went past. To my amazement, there were shelves lined with books. The only book we had was the Bible. There isn't much room for books in a covered wagon—just food, clothes and necessities—but even at home in Vermont, we didn't have books in the house.

A tall girl with brown hair and eyes was setting the table in the dining room. "Hello, I'm Elsa. You're wanted in the kitchen to help fix supper. The cook is sick and Mrs. Coffer's nervous as a cat."

Elsa was solid of body and face with red cheeks. She spoke with a slight lisp.

I trudged into the small stuffy room behind the larger dining room. "Here, Lucy. Peel the potatoes." My mistress spoke sharply. She looked at me and must have seen my watery eyes. "Before you do, here's a bit of candy. The sugar will pick you up for now as you won't have time to eat until after the guests are served." She put two pieces of taffy in my hand. Now, we only ever had candy on grand occasions, so that was an unexpected treat. Maybe she was like Ma—kind, but no foolishness. I began to feel at home.

During dinner, I peeked into the dining room. The officers were in uniform and the ladies all had on nice but no-nonsense wool dresses. They had wine at the table in lovely delicate glasses. If I left the door open just a crack, I could hear them talking. I quietly washed the dinner dishes while they had dessert. I was very careful not to break any of the fancy china.

Major Coffer was speaking, "I'm not too worried about the Indians and the English attacking. You remember how the British incited the chiefs of the Miamis to fight General Wayne back in 1794. Even though Chief Little Turtle wanted to discuss peace, he was outvoted. So they fought at Fallen Timbers. When the Indians were overcome by the American troops, they went to the British at Fort Miami for protection. But the Brits closed the gates and left them at the mercy of their enemy. No, I don't think the Indians will join the Brits again."

A tall red-haired officer they called John Howell spoke up, "That may be, but only eleven Northwestern tribes signed the Greenville Treaty after the battle at Fallen Timbers. The Shawnee chief, Tecumseh, would not sign. He's a very important chief. Rumor has it that Tecumseh is visiting other tribes up and down the territory trying to unify the tribes. He knows he can't trust the British, but he likes the Americans even less. As for the Brits, I think they're still smarting from the Revolution. They're taking over American ships, kidnapping American sailors and acting like we are still subjects of the king. Mark my words, it won't be more than a few years before we'll have another war with Britain, and I wouldn't be surprised if the Indians were to join them against us yet again."

Major Coffer laughed. "Would you place a wager on that, John?"

"Yes, Sir, a month's pay!"

Elsa had served the dessert while I scrubbed the pots. We both looked up when Mrs. Coffer stepped into the kitchen. "Lucy, we're going to take our coffee into the parlor. Please clear the table and finish the dishes. Help yourself to the leftovers. Elsa can join you."

The military were big eaters I thought. Not a lot of food was left over, but Elsa and I managed to scrape together enough to feel satisfied. The turkey was all gone but lots of dressing was left, cooked carrots and spinach. Elsa spoke with her mouth full of bread, "Don't you think that Captain Howell is the handsomest man you ever saw?"

"I couldn't see him very well, but I sure heard him say the Indians might attack." I started doing up the dessert plates.

"Well, when my time for getting married comes, I plan to marry a military man and travel around a lot," she exclaimed. I paid her no heed. My thoughts were on Tecumseh.

Two weeks later, Mrs. Coffer found me examining the books while I was dusting the parlor. "Do you know how to read, Lucy?"

I was embarrassed. "Yes, of course, Ma'am. We don't have a lot of books at home, just the family Bible. But we all in our family learned how to read and do sums early on. I was just admiring all of your books."

Her manner softened just a little. "Whenever you get done with your chores, you may come in here and read some. Just don't take the books out of this room or get any food on them. The Major and I are going out for dinner this evening. If you wish, you may go home this afternoon and spend the night. Just be back early in the morning in time to milk the cow and do the breakfast dishes."

I could hardly wait to tie up my few things and start off. Darkness was coming as I ran the last half-mile. Ma was making stew on one of the outdoor fires but turned when she heard my eager footsteps.

"Lucy, what are you doing home? Are you sick? Did Mrs. Coffer let you go?"

"I'm fine, Ma. They were going out for the evening, so she suggested I could come home if I was back early tomorrow morning." Only then did Ma hug me.

"Minerva is here too," Ma smiled. "Seems there's some big military dinner, and she has the night off. It'll be good to hear what all you girls have to tell. Pa's doing well clearing the land. He promised he'd have a cabin laid up to the chamber floor by January. He's got to split out some shingles—they call 'em clapboards here—for the upper floor, and we can move in. He's trying to finish up quick to save on our boarding fees. Come on in, you're just in time for supper." Ma piled the stew into a big kettle.

I started to follow her into the little square house, but Pa showed up and dumped an armload of logs outside the door. He gave me a big bear hug. "I've missed my Lucy!" he growled. I felt the world was right.

Pa had fashioned some split logs across a couple of stumps for a makeshift table and more logs across lower stumps for benches. The table was set with our familiar wooden trenchers and pewter plates. I felt right at home. Minerva came over and hugged me as soon as I walked in the door. Even Cyrus and Thomas seemed happy to see me.

Seated at the table after supper, Ma asked, "Girls, tell us all your news."

Minerva mused, "Well, I have news of Becky. After I cook a meal and it's all cleaned up, I can walk about some outside for exercise. So I often go over to see how Becky's coming on her sewing. It seems the Treadwells don't have any children. Mostly she's making clothes for Mrs. Treadwell. They've really taken a shine to Becky, treat her like a daughter. She told them the light isn't too good up in the room where she sleeps. So she asked could she sew in the parlor. She promised to leave if anyone came calling. So here's little Miss Seamstress all set up in the parlor, pretty as you please, looking industrious with her yellow curls in plain view through the parlor window. It seems Mr. Treadwell does a lot of business in his office next to the parlor at home. A certain Capt. John Howell comes to call, sees Becky and presto he's hooked! Now he comes regularly on some pretext or other. To put a top on it, he's a cultured Southerner! Something she always wanted!" She laughed gleefully.

We all laughed except Pa and Ma, who exchanged worried looks. "I think I'd better look in on Becky," Ma declared.

Minerva continued, "There's more. A few weeks later, Henry Wolcott, a young farmer from Vermont came to visit Mr. Treadwell on some business about Ohio becoming a state. He no sooner sees Becky sewing when, lo and behold, he's visiting regularly too."

I exclaimed, "I saw Captain Howell. He had dinner at the Coffers. He thinks we're going to have to fight the British again. Maybe even in just a few years!" I remembered I'd seen a book about states' rights at the Coffers. "Pa, is Ohio going to become a state?" I asked.

"Well, we hope so. For many years, Mr. Arthur St. Clair was governor of the Northwest Territory. At first he did a good job. A legislature was formed and a tax system set up. William Henry Harrison was elected as a delegate to Congress, and two years ago he proposed the Harrison Land Act. It passed and established offices where people could buy land. So more people came west, people like us. Now with all these people and this big territory, everyone feels the territory has to be divided up so it can become a couple of big states or several smaller states.

"That's where the trouble comes in. Where to put the dividing lines? St. Clair wants the territory divided along the Scioto River," Pa explained. "But Mr. Thomas Worthington led a group that pushed to keep the divisions designated by the Northwest Ordinance. Congress passed the Ordinance just last year, in 1800. We still have some work to do setting up the boundaries, so for now we have to wait and see what happens next. Mr. St. Clair has become old and grumpy and seems to be opposed to statehood for Ohio. I'm afraid he's not long for the office of Governor."

"How do you like the Coffers, Lucy," Minerva asked.

"Mrs. Coffer is nice but stern. She doesn't put up with any foolishness. They have shelves of books in their parlor. Mrs. Coffer volunteered I could read them if I get all my chores done and don't get food on the books."

"Books are valuable. Don't you damage any books, Lucy, or we'll have to pay for them," Ma warned.

"Yes, Ma." I turned to Pa. "When can we all get to the new house, Pa?"

"We'll be together by spring," Pa swore.

The next morning I left before sunup. I didn't mind so much going back to the Coffers' since I knew what it was like there. I think the scariest things are the ones that are new, unknown—ones that you can only imagine. Still, I was already looking forward to spring and going home to my family.

CHAPTER ELEVEN

NEW BEGINNINGS

January and February away from my family dragged by. The weather, though, was milder than in Vermont. The roads were dusty like summertime most of the winter. In fact, it didn't seem much like winter at all. We did have several light snowfalls in late January and early February, but the snow came at night and was gone by mid-morning. I missed the sledding, but the warm weather meant Pa could build the house faster.

Both Ma and Eliza wrote news of the family every few days, and Minerva stopped by to see me when she could. Eliza's notes assured me that she and Squire Prouty had arrived safely with all the horses. They were secure and safe in rented rooms. She and her Ezra had bought some land, and he was busy setting up a blacksmith shop. Ma's letters filled me with joy. With the help of Mr. Stacey and the Squire, Pa had put three more rounds of logs on the house and had added a roof. Pa helped them in turn, but they aimed to finish Pa's house first since he had a family to gather back together. In as much time as they could spare, they cleared land for all three so they could start planting in the spring.

I could sense Ma's happiness when she wrote that she and the younger children had been able to move into the house as soon as it was finished up to the chamber floor. Ma celebrated when Pa got the fireplace built. Her letters told of how he'd measured off the space for it and cut out the wood from the walls to match that shape., After he'd laid stones to fill in the space, he'd checked again and again to be sure there was a good draft.

Minerva brightened a dreary February day when she stopped by to tell me that I could move home at the end of March. When I told Mrs. Coffer that I would be leaving come spring, she was very kind. "I'll miss you. Lucy," she exclaimed with a slight tremor in her voice. "You're a good worker, well mannered and quiet. If ever you want to come back, you are welcome. I do hope you'll come visit me from time to time."

I felt a certain sadness to be leaving her, and especially to be leaving her books. The day I bid good-bye she took me into the parlor and handed me a leather-bound volume. "This is to remember me by." I was struck dumb. It was *Gulliver's Travels* by Jonathan Swift and had been published in England. I knew it was incredibly valuable. She hugged me. No one outside our family ever had hugged me, and absolutely no one ever had given me a book. I hugged her back.

"Thank you so very much, Mrs. Coffer. I've never had a book all my own. I'll take good care of it, and I'll visit you often. If ever you need me to help, I'll be glad to come. You won't have to pay me. I feel like you're family." We both cried a bit and wiped our eyes. I packed up my bundle and precious book, said farewell to Elsa, and started to our new home. For once I didn't mind the long walk.

As I ran up to the house, I could see that the pear trees were in full bloom. Mr. Bingham, the farmer whose land adjoined ours, had planted his acreage in apple and peach trees. Pa had purchased an additional eight acres from Mr. Bingham, when he learned the old man was going back to Rhode Island to live near his son. We'd had an apple orchard in Vermont, but I had never seen peach trees. For a moment, their wonderful fragrant blooms stopped me in my tracks.

When, at last, I burst through the door, Ma gave me a surprisingly fierce hug. "let me show you about our sturdy new home" She was as proud as if she was showing off a palace. Compared to the square blockhouse, it *was* a palace. Everything was clean and fresh inside, and it smelled of new-sawn wood. The spacious main room, with its huge fireplace and hearth, reminded me of our house in Vermont. Next to it was a bedroom for Ma and Pa. And we had stairs instead of a ladder! Where we had a loft in Vermont, here there was a second story divided into three airy rooms. The cutout windows all over the house had shutters, but no glass yet.

"Lucy, this is the room you'll share with Eva and with little Claire, when she's big enough. One of the other rooms is for the boys. The third is for Abby, Becky and Sarah. Pa hasn't had time to make any furniture yet. He wants to put up a barn for some cattle, and he also wants to help Squire Prouty finish his house and Mr. Stacey his. Put your things down now and come to supper." For a woman of few words, that was quite a speech for Ma the longest I could remember.

After she went downstairs to finish up the cooking, I walked to the first bedroom window I'd ever had. I looked out over the rich brown of the newly tilled fields, over the young fruit trees and all the way to the river. So high up, I felt as if I were in the sky playing at being an angel. But I knew I was no angel.

There was great excitement as we gathered for our first evening meal together in our new home. Even Mr. Stacey had a place at the table. He'd been taking meals with our family ever since he'd started working so closely with Pa and the Squire. Each of us in turn had a tale to tell.

After we gave thanks, Abby started off: "I really liked that family I was with, but taking care of three small children and a frail mother is very tiring. I'm ever so happy to get back to weaving, making meals and working for my own family again. That reminds me, Pa. Will you build us a loom so we can start weaving? We'll have to buy the wool since we didn't bring any sheep to Ohio. Or maybe we can trade and get the wool in return for weaving some of it up."

"You know, I just might be able to do that," Pa agreed. "I could work on a loom at night when it's too dark to build on Stacey or Prouty's places. Some of the folk around here will be shearing their sheep soon, so I'd best get to it. I plan to buy some lambs this spring, and we can have our own wool by next year."

"Ma. Ma!" Becky interrupted, self-absorbed as usual. "I made some friends while I was sewing at the Treadwells. They asked if they could call on me. Would that be all right?" We all looked surprised. Becky enjoyed her moment of importance.

"Who are they?" Ma inquired.

Becky preened like a peacock. "One is John Howell. He's a captain in the military at Fort Campus Martius. The other is Henry Woolcott. He's from Vermont. His father and brother own some land around here. He's bought some land himself and is interested in the politics of the area."

"Of course, your friends are welcome here," Ma replied. "I would like to meet them. Sundays are good visiting days."

"I think Sarah will be having a gentleman caller soon, too. William Putnam kept coming by to see how she was doing," Minerva confided. Sarah blushed.

"What about you, Minerva," Becky asked with a knowing smirk. "Have you met any gentlemen?"

Ignoring Becky's intended slight, Minerva took a deep breath. "I've been thinking. I would like to go to the normal school being set up here and train to become a teacher!"

"A girl teacher! Well I never!" Becky sputtered.

Mr. Stacey had been quiet all evening, respectful of our family's eagerness to exchange news and lay out plans for the future. At Becky's outburst, though, he raised his head and uttered two powerful words: "Why not?" Before they had died away, he continued: "Minerva is the brightest student I've ever had. She can spell better than anyone, even me." He stared pointedly at Becky who had trouble writing a letter. "She knows her arithmetic just as well as some of my friends who teach."

In the instant that Pa hesitated, Ma spoke up, her eyes shining: "Of course you can go, Minerva. I think it's fine for you to want to be a teacher. We're mighty proud of you to be able to aspire to that. Aren't we, Pa?"

What could Pa add? Whatever he may have thought, he hesitated no more. "Your mother's right, Minerva. We'll find a way for you to go to school, although you may have to work to help pay the way."

"Now, Lucy, it's your turn," Minerva cried.

"Just a minute," I called out as I ran upstairs to get the book Mrs. Coffer had given me. Carrying my precious gift, I was careful on my way back downstairs. "When I left today, Mrs. Coffer gave me this book!" I held it up for all to see. They exchanged glances and sighed with admiration, for they could tell it was as valuable as it was beautiful. I went on, "It's from England! Mrs. Coffer said she wanted me to come back and visit. I promised I'd help her for free if ever she needed me, and that I thought of her like one of the family."

"Honey, that's a mighty fine book and right expensive. Why don't we keep it with the Bible so it's safe," Ma exclaimed when I paused for breath.

I was disappointed. I'd wanted to keep it by my bed so I could touch it before I went to sleep. "Can I read it when I want?" I asked.

"Gosh!" Thomas whooped. "Maybe some day you'll be a famous writer!" Everyone laughed.

"Don't laugh! She just might be," Ma asserted. "Yes, of course you can read it when you want to. Now let's get the dishes done and the chores finished."

I took my book and quietly went outside. I hid under the peach trees and looked up at the evening sky. The fragrance of blossoms overhead was all around me. A soft wind blew some petals against my cheek. They were soft as chicks' down. Heaven must be like this, I thought. I closed my eyes and wished that time would stop and that the world would never change. I heard voices near me. Abby and Mr. Stacey had walked out into the orchard too. I scrunched down and tried to be very quiet so they wouldn't know I was there, when I should have been out doing chores. They were standing very close together.

"Abby," Mr. Stacey said almost in a whisper, "you must know how I feel about you even though I've never had the nerve to speak. You're so pretty and smart. I'm so poor and ugly, but I love you. Do you think you could . . . that is would . . . you consider . . . that is . . . would you marry me?" He gulped. I imagined his Adam's apple going up and down and thought, he's right about one thing. He is ugly! But he has been a great help. I hope she says "no" in such a way as not to hurt his feelings.

"You're not ugly, my dear man," Abby replied. "Not to me. And I would be proud to marry you. I love you too, Matthew, and I think we can make a very good living together. We're neither of us afraid to work. And I think you're very kind and brave. Just like the way you stood up for Minerva just now. Or the way you helped time and again when we were on the river and all along the trail. You and I may never be rich—or we may—but that's not the most important thing."

I scrunched down further, flabbergasted! "I can't believe you said yes." Mr. Stacey stuttered. *I couldn't believe it either!* Sweet, kind, beautiful Abby marry that teacher! "Life has always been hard for me," he added without any self-pity in his voice, "but I've loved you ever since that first day I saw you. I told myself not to dream, yet when you were so kind to me and seemed interested, I dared hope." He paused, seemed to gather strength and plunged on: "I should have the house done by August and the crops in and harvested. We can be married then. I want to have a house to take you to. I've saved my earnings and the money from my farm, so we'll have a little something to start on. I only wish I had more to give you. You deserve more. I'm not eloquent, Abby, and I'm saying this badly, but I promise I'll be a good husband."

"I'll be perfectly happy to be your wife." Abby murmured. I couldn't hear what they said. They may have been kissing.

"I'll speak to your father tomorrow," he confided with quiet confidence. "You've made me so happy."

"We'd best get back, Matthew," Abby replied. "Mother will need help getting the youngsters to bed. She looks tired."

I lay back on the grass under the trees. Everything had been so perfect just a few minutes earlier. But marriage meant Abby would be leaving in August. Things never would be the same. I somehow hadn't felt that way when Eliza left. She seemed so much older and distanced from me. But Abby stood up for me. She comforted me. Why couldn't time have stopped several minutes back? I wallowed in my despair for a few minutes more and trudged back to the house.

The next day Mr. Stacey asked Pa for Abby's hand, and everyone knew that they were to be married. When Pa and Ma were alone that night, I got all my courage up and went in to talk with them. "Why is Abby marrying that poor teacher? She's so much kinder than Becky and smarter and, I think, prettier. But I bet Becky will marry one of her rich beaus and have an easy life. Why does Abby have to get married at all? It's not fair!"

Ma looked up from her knitting. "Who ever told you life was fair? Wherever did you get that idea?"

Pa smiled at me. "Come here, Lucy." I went over and sat on a low bench beside him. "Honey, people can lose their money and their position. If you marry for wealth, you may end up with a poor man who had no other value but money and find you got a bad bargain. But if you marry a hard worker, an honest man, intelligent and kind, you have a better chance at happiness. I'm going to start that loom tomorrow. That way Abby can earn a little to help out when she and Matthew start keeping house."

Pa was as good as his word. Within a few days, working late into the night, he had a loom ready to be dressed. And, in no time at all, Ma had procured wool that we quickly carded and spun. So within two weeks, the older girls were working on the loom. When Pa promised he'd make another loom to keep us all busy, I knew it wouldn't be long before I would have a chance to do some weaving myself.

One day Ma asked Abby to make a piece of cloth for a woman who had promised butter in return. When the cloth was finished, Ma called, "Lucy I want you to deliver this piece for me and bring back the butter."

"But Ma," I protested, "it's two miles through the woods! No one lives between here and there, I'll get lost!" A large forest surrounded our farm for miles. Once lost in there, a person would be hard to find . . . ever.

"Nonsense! You're a big girl of twelve now. Just keep between the hill and the river. It'll be the first house you come to. Take the canoe to get across the river."

We never argued with Ma, so I started out. Our family always kept a canoe at the shore to cross the river. I'd never piloted it by myself, and the paddle shook in my hands. When I landed on the other side, there wasn't a road—only a footpath. The woods were dark, so I tried to walk quickly. Perhaps because there was no one was in sight, I remembered the stories of Indians capturing lone walkers. Snap! A branch cracked, and I walked faster. I was so keyed up that when a squirrel scampered across my path, I nearly died. Tall trees shadowed the sun. I stopped for a minute, and a snake glided within a few inches of my foot. That did it! I started to run. Finally I heard a rooster crowing and sheep bleating. Thank heaven, the house was near!

A sweet lady with mouse-colored hair called out, "Hey there, are you the Howe girl?" She was standing back from a fence, hanging clothes to dry on the rails.

"Yes, Ma'am. Ma said you had some butter to trade for this cloth." Relief must have showed in my voice.

"Would you like a bite before you start back?" she called over her shoulder as she went to the springhouse to fetch the butter.

"No, thank you. I'd best get back real quick. Ma has chores for me." All I could think about all the way home was that family living all alone in the woods. What must they think about at night so far away from everyone when the wolves and coyotes howled? But I had done it! I had walked in the woods by myself. Somehow I walked a little taller, at my regular pace and I wasn't scared anymore.

One morning in early summer after all the crops had been planted, Matthew Stacey came by. He often dropped in casually since he was almost one of the family. Working outside had tanned his pale skin, and he spoke and walked with a new confidence. "How would the children like to take a picnic lunch and go see the Indian mounds in Marietta?" he asked.

Ma perked up. "I think that's a fine idea. I'd like to go along myself." So we all set to work packing a big box with food and jugs of cider. I felt like we were on holiday. We piled into the wagon and drove to some of the mounds. They were located all over Marietta.

First we went to a place called Conus Mound. We sat in the wagon and looked at a strange cone shape. Mr. Stacey in his best schoolteacher voice began: "This large burial mound was put up by ancient Indians probably thousands of years ago. When the first settlers came here, they decided to name all the mounds as public places and decreed that they would be preserved. There are known to be a multitude of mounds throughout the territory. A man from Marietta told me he had seen one mound that was sixty-eight feet high. The ancient Indians of the Ohio territory built it. I just hope other cities and counties are saving their mounds. This cone and the land around it were designated as a cemetery. Last year Mound Cemetery was officially founded"

"How do they know it's a burial place? Did they find any bodies?" Cyrus demanded.

"No. I don't know if they ever will search for bodies. How would you like them to dig up your grandparent's graves? If they do excavate, I hope they do it carefully and not just go in searching for trinkets. We call it a burial ground because that's what the Indians called it. Let's go to the next one. We can have a picnic there." As we drove off, I looked over my shoulder, imagining I was a young Indian walking away from my grandparent's place of rest. I was glad they had preserved it.

The Quadranaou Mound was a three-acre area. We jumped down from the wagon, and Ma spread a blanket on the grass. Abby and Becky put out platters of bread and fruit, meat and jugs of cider. Mr. Stacey continued his talk as we ate. "The Indians tell us this was an ancient ceremonial place for the Hopewell Indians. The place we'll pass on the way home was called the Sacred Way. It was a walled walk from here to the Ohio River. Sad to tell, some of the settlers have begun taking away some of the wall material. There are other mounds they call effigy mounds that resemble large animals or snakes."

"Could it be that some of these mounds were just tall places where the Indians could build fires and make smoke to communicate with each other?" Minerva asked.

"Could be. Or it could be that, unbeknownst to us, they had studied the stars and used these places to track their movements. Someday we may find out."

"Were the Indians that smart?" Becky asked.

"We underestimate the Indians," he replied. "They were successfully growing crops and had a form of government that worked well. It was just different from ours."

After we'd finished eating, we got back in the wagon and drove home. As we passed the Sacred Way, I tried to imagine what it would be like to live in a bark house and be outdoors most of the time. I would have liked that life, I thought, and when I die, maybe I can come back as an Indian, or maybe in this life, when I grow up, I could join the Indians.

Summer passed quickly. We were busy getting in the crops and preparing for Abby's wedding. She had woven a light-colored very fine linen for her dress. And every few days she added something to the store of items—things she'd need for her new life—in her small hope chest. In the last few days before the ceremony, Ma nearly killed herself—and us girls too—preparing food and cleaning. Pa wisely took Cyrus and Thomas into the fields where they'd be out from underfoot.

The morning of the wedding dawned at last, and I roamed the fields and along hedgerows picking wildflowers for Abby to carry. Our pastor performed the ceremony in front of the fireplace in our new home. As they repeated their vows, Abby in her beautiful dress and Mr. Stacey in a nicely cut jacket and *new boots*, were radiant. Most of the women, including Ma, dabbed at their eyes, but Clara Putnam, surprisingly, wore a lovely smile. And I admit to smiling too, because I found that I was truly happy for my sister.

Ma had invited the three families who'd journeyed with us from Vermont, some friends who had come out to Ohio earlier than we did and some new neighbors from along the Muskingum. When Abby threw her bouquet, though, Becky was the lucky girl who caught it. She laughed and predicted: "I'm going to get married in December at Christmas."

Sarah, always the romantic, beamed. "Who will you marry, Becky? Both of your young men seem to be in love with you."

"That's easy," Minerva answered. "She'll marry the richer one!"

After the wedding supper, Abby and her new husband drove off in his wagon. Matthew—I had been invited to call him by his first name as he had become my "brother"—had finished his house. We were going to see it the next afternoon. But before she left, Abby whispered to me, "Lucy, you can come see us whenever you want . . . and stay overnight too."

That evening, too full of the excitement of Abby's special day to go to sleep, I sat on the front porch bench until the moon rose high in the night sky. Pa came out and sat beside me. "A penny for your thoughts, Lucy."

"I was thinking, Pa, you're right. The moon shines here just like it does in Vermont."

He laughed. "Lucy, the moon will shine for you wherever you go."

"I think it will, Pa. I think it will."

4478240R00081

Made in the USA
San Bernardino, CA
22 September 2013